FIELD GUIDE TO THE AMERICAN TEENAGER
A SURVIVAL GUIDE FOR PARENTS

By
Jerome C. Vergamini, MD and Ray Miskimins, Ph.D.

Aurora Books
Eugene, Oregon, USA

Aurora Books, an imprint of Eco-Justice Press, L.L.C.

Aurora Books
P.O. Box 5409 Eugene, OR 97405
www.ecojusticepress.com

Field Guide To The American Teenager:
A Survival Guide For Parents

By Jerome C. Vergamini, MD and Ray Miskimins, Ph.D.

Cover by David Diethelm, Eco-Justice Press
Cover photo © Rido / Adobe Stock

Library of Congress Control Number: 2016952579
ISBN 978-1-945432-09-5

TABLE OF CONTENTS

FORWARD

One evening a number of years ago, two mental health professionals away from their offices on a steelhead fishing vacation decided to put their heads together to collaborate on a book about teens. The result of that decision is what you are now reading! Between us we estimated that we had over 50 years of experience in working with children, adolescents and their families. And we realized that we had not yet found a practical book on the market that supplied parents with a reasonable resource of information, one that would help them to understand their teens and to deal with them comfortably and effectively. By combining the training, perspective and experience of a psychiatrist and a psychologist, both specializing in work with adolescents, we felt that a broad consideration of all the important issues would be possible. We decided to try to put that missing book together and began to work on it. We spent many hours planning, outlining, and writing the first few chapters. Then there were interruptions. One of us moved to another state, and the work had to be shared by email, phone and travel, but we managed to finish.

This book was written in an effort to share our combined knowledge of teens, gained both as mental health professionals and as parents. We wanted to put together something that parents could understand, short and to the point, with as little psychological jargon as possible, and most importantly, something that would be useful. Our planning began with a look at the various aspects of the teenage experience that regularly impact upon parenting. We decided to include information on development, communication, schools, peer relationships, families, sexuality, religion, drugs and alcohol, and mental health problems, and to attempt to frame everything around these subjects. Throughout the book we have brought our different perspectives into play. Dr. Vergamini, a child and adolescent psychiatrist, has for several decades consulted to many child and adolescent evaluation and/or treatment programs (inpatient, outpatient, mental health, substance abuse, etc.) and operated a private medical practice (in Oregon). Dr. Miskimins, a clinical psychologist, draws from his experiences directing an inner-city program for youth in Colorado, serving as Clinical Director (then as Executive Director) of an adolescent residential treatment center for emotionally disturbed teens in Oregon, and maintaining a long-term private practice. In addition, both of us are family men, still married to the same women we started out with, and each has three children, now grown. And each of us has had a child with special needs.

The purpose of this book is to give some basic information on the most important topics relating to parenting teenagers. We also have tried to provide some resources to help parents when it is needed beyond the scope of this book. The Field Guide cannot be an encyclopedia, but can be a starting place to begin knowing more about teens and to try to bridge the gap between parent's own memories of what that was like and the changing times. We will try to give examples where we can. We will attempt to anticipate questions, but we know there may be gaps. For this reason, in our last chapter we will discuss some means to get some help with some of your questions which we may have not answered in this book. We would like you to keep this in mind as you read, and to jot down questions that you may have or information that you seek, so that we or others can address those issues for you. As you read on, the questions may be answered, or they may raise further questions.

Adolescence is an intriguing time. For some reasons that we may not always understand, adults may tend to treat teens as mysterious creatures, a group of people that are difficult to fathom. Maybe it is because of how they band together, or their peculiar use of language, or their strange dress codes, or the seemingly constant protesting, or their tendency to test limits, but it might be because adults have developed some amnesia for the trials and tribulations of that time in their own lives. If you can't remember what being a teenager trying to grow up in this society was like, then you are likely to see the current crop of adolescents as creatures that can't be understood, and therefore to be feared. It is much like some of us fear spiders, because they have eight legs and move fast, and we don't know much about them except that a few are dangerous.

Understanding and remembering is the reason that we write this book. We hope to inform adults enough about the teenagers around them, that they do not have to be uneasy or fearful when they deal with them. We want parents to enjoy them, laugh with them, revel in their successes, and help them through their failures. We want adults to appreciate their pains and their joys, and comfortably relate to their kids through both. Ultimately we want them to grow up, survive, and be good citizens. We want them to sometimes be like us and sometimes not be like us.

As you read through this book we hope you enjoy our efforts to you with information about teenagers. We trust that jumping into this subject with both feet will stimulate and educate you, and maybe resurrect some memory of your own existence as a kid. We hope that our experiences with teens can prove useful not only in anticipating and understanding yours, but in learning to take joy in them. We would like this book to impact both your knowledge and your attitudes, making your job of raising kids easier, sounder, and lot more fun.

Chapter I
INTRODUCTION

"O, Wonder! How many goodly creatures are here!
How beauteous mankind is! O Brave new world,
That has such people in't!"
— "The Tempest" by William Shakespeare

I had a friend who had a new child, and his older brother, about 6 years old, was attracting concern from his teacher because, though he enjoyed drawing pictures, they were all colored in black. The teacher, being concerned about depression or other adjustment issues because of the new baby brother, recommended that the parents see a mental health practitioner with the child. As a result, I had a visit with the youngster and I suggested we do some drawing. Sure enough, he chose the color black to do his picture. I said to him, "Boy, you sure like black, don't you?" He replied, "Yes, it's the same color as licorice, and that's my favorite candy!" It turned out that he was actually quite thrilled to have a baby brother.

While working in a mental health clinic, I was referred a young man about 15 years old, who was angry about coming in to see me, and who insisted that he was not going to take any medication. "I'm not depressed and don't need to take any medicine." After calming him down by my *refusing* to give him any medicine, even if he changed his mind, I suggested we just talk about what he was so upset and angry about. It turned out that he was living with his grandfather, who was careful to track his behavior and activities and who was appearing to do a pretty good job of keeping this youth up on his schoolwork and chores. However, the young man was upset that he could not live with his mother. She had relinquished custody to the grandfather some years before, the reasons not being that clear. I continued to meet with him about monthly for a number of times to just talk, until he came in one day and said, "I know that I am really depressed, and I wonder if it wouldn't be a good idea to put me on an antidepressant medicine." I did so and he got somewhat better, but still obsessed about getting back to his mother. When I said I would talk to the grandfather about maybe spending some time with her, he said, "He'll never go along with that." However, by this time, the grandfather was ready to give anything a try, and we arranged to have him alternate living with grandfather for a week and mother for a week. The boy was blown away about my powers of persuasion. In about 2 months, the boy came back to me and said, "I think it's not working out at my mother's house. I think I should just go back to live with my grandfather." We switched back, he stopped taking the medicine, and he proceeded to do well in high school and eventually to graduate.

I and my wife, Judy, a professional counselor, were working with a young 16 year old boy who had been raised in a Russian orphanage. He had been adopted by a family in this country and was having some adjustment issues. Judy was doing most of the face to face work with him. One day they were about to start, but I was about to take a break and to go and get a cup of coffee. I poked my head in and asked Judy if she would like a cup of hot chocolate on my return. She said she would, and I asked the young man if he would like one too. He looked surprised and finally nodded that he would. When I left to go get them, he looked at Judy and said, "Why did he do that?" He had a hard time grasping that a psychiatrist would just do something friendly. It was the beginning of his gradually being able to trust us.

Parents tend to think of children, especially as they reach their teens, as enigmatic. Just what is going on in their heads? If you think back to when you were 18 – 20 years old, you realize that you have much more experience in a variety of life situations now than you did then and would probably do many things differently than you did then. Think of kids in a similar way. A toddler tends to explore things around him/her, but is constantly checking to see if Mom or Dad is still around and frequently toddles back to the parent to physically check in. Teens are much the same, though their world is much more global than the living room. However they are constantly going out, first in groups, then more singly, to check out the world, but then returning to the safety and security of the home and family, sometimes checking in quietly, other times openly talking about their experiences. They are accumulating experience to be able to use now and as they get older. Understanding our kids in this context helps us to better teach them how to sort things out and to make better decisions. Just like exploring helps them to trust their environment, we also need to help them to trust us to provide good advice and the right amount of confidence that allows them to do so successfully.

It is important to remember that most adolescents are good kids who are just in a new phase of their lives—they are just growing up. For every teenager who murders, rapes, or robs banks, there are literally thousands who create no problems of note for anyone, and are soon to be productive, functioning members of our society. They are the future. The bad stuff we read about kids in the papers is far overshadowed by the great stuff that kids do. However, all of us do make mistakes in the process of learning. It is important to remember that mistakes are the way we learn, whether they are things like throwing a ball in the kitchen and breaking a favorite cup, forgetting to relay a phone message so that mom misses an important meeting, or dating the wrong girl and getting heartbroken. As parents, a most important task for us is to minimize the opportunity our children have for really bad choices, those with really bad consequences. Leaving kids completely to fend for themselves is like putting your son or daughter behind the wheel of an automobile before they have any idea of how to drive or have learned the rules of the road. They need your help before they step on the gas pedal.

As you read through the rest of this book we hope you enjoy our efforts to provide you with information about teenagers. We trust that jumping into this subject with both feet will stimulate and educate you, and maybe resurrect some memory of your own existence as a kid. We hope that our experiences with teens can prove useful not only in anticipating and understanding yours, but in learning to take joy in them. We would like this book to affect both your knowledge and your attitudes, making your job of raising kids easier, sounder, and lot more fun.

Chapter 2
GROWTH AND DEVELOPMENT

"Two roads diverged in a wood, and I – I took the one less
traveled by, And that has made all the difference."
— **Robert Frost "The Road Not Taken"**

Almost everyone has a favorite relative somewhere, one that only visits once or twice a year. And every parent has heard, "My Gosh, Kevin is growing", from that relative on almost every visit. "He must be a foot taller than last summer, and he's becoming such a gentleman." The first half of that statement refers to his growing body; the second half refers to his growing personality. That brings us to an important proposition: Everyone from newborn to death is growing "psychologically". In adults, because they are no longer physically getting larger, it is sometimes not very obvious, but the changes in personality are seen in "mid-life crises", divorces, moving to new interests, returning to school, and so on. However, in kids, change is very clear to everyone (including the kids) and is punctuated by the simple routine of raising the mark on the wall showing their height.

To help you understand your teenagers and their changes, we will talk a lot in this book about issues like communication, sex, peer relations, school, and so on, but always bearing in mind that, to some extent, what is happening for your child regarding these issues is in part dependent upon his or her level of psychological development. As adults, we must always moderate our expectations of our kids, in all areas, from social skills to helping with work around the house, based upon the child's age. Simply stated, we expect more of older kids than we do of younger ones.

We usually find that the older the child is, the further along they will be in all the various aspects of personality development (like intellectual skills, social skills, self perception, and so on).

A few months ago, a man and woman came to our office for a consultation regarding their "problem child". They frantically described their teenage boy, an only child, who was "scared to death of girls". When asked to elaborate, they said that he had never been on a "real date", that he had told them that he found it extremely "hard to think of something to say" when alone with a girl, and that he was "real nervous" about an upcoming dance class in P.E. at school. This all sounded rather serious, because we had understood their boy to be a sophomore or junior in college. At age eighteen or nineteen, a little tension is expected, but to be nearly incapacitated by fear could require some professional help. With one question the whole picture changed: "How old is David?" When the parents answered, "thirteen", the rest of the session was devoted to helping them to understand adolescent development. The "problems" they had sketched are common for his age group, and there was no crisis. As parents, they simply needed to give their son a lot of understanding and encouragement sprinkled with a little information relevant to the tensions of dealing with the opposite sex.

Any evaluation of or interaction with your kids should always take into account their level of growth and development. Think back about yourself and how you thought and acted five years, ten years, or twenty years ago. You will realize that you have changed some, and believe it or not, you continue to change. Can you remember some of your idealism when you were a teen? Now you are probably more practical and pragmatic. Can you remember your interests of past years? Some have changed. You may spend more time watching sports now than participating, and you may easily tire of talk about diapers and baby food. You probably spend little or no time dancing, and may think of a car as transportation. You probably care little about what kind of shoes everyone else is wearing unless they look very comfortable. You and all the adults around you continue to change; so do teenagers, but teen changes are much more obvious and much more profound. What happens to you in several years can happen to your kids in a few months. This chapter will give you the highlights of what we, as parents, all need to keep in mind about our children's growth and development. The information here sets the foundation for the rest of the information contained in this book.

Normality

Before we launch into discussions in various areas of childhood development, we will pause and talk about the concept of "normal". Any look at psychological growth in your children brings that concept into play—are they coming along at an expected rate or are they lagging behind. People are always asking us if their teenagers' behaviors are "normal". At first glance, this may seem like a simple, very straightforward question to ask a mental health professional. However, nothing could be further from the truth. We must look at is the meaning of the word "normal". Much has been written, many studies have been completed, and the experts have many opinions about normality, so we would like you to consider this concept in some depth.

Normal can be viewed from at least four different perspectives:

1) *Normal as statistical.* Statistical normal means what most individuals do in a given situation. If 90% of the population sleeps 8 hours per night, that is normal. If 90% of Lemmings rush to their deaths into the ocean once every 5 years, that is normal Lemming behavior. Choosing not to suicide in this case is "abnormal". If all Lemmings were "normal", that would be the end of Lemmings, so some of them must stay home and let the others go rushing off. Some of them choose statistically abnormal behavior. Thomas Edison only slept a few hours each night and caught catnaps during the day. That made him abnormal. As you can see from these examples, being abnormal does not necessarily equate to being "bad". Statistical normal is a way we can compare ourselves or our children against the rest of the population, but it is something we need to look at very carefully before we assign value judgments of "good" or "bad".

2) *Normal as ideal* (utopian). Some people view normal as what is optimal or best, even if it is pretty much unattainable. Sigmund

Freud, for example, would have classified many behaviors that would be considered statistically normal as abnormal (not that Freud was correct about all things). Looking at some religious tenets provides another example— masturbation is very common among adolescent boys and thus statistically normal, but some would say that any engagement in this activity is not normal. In this case they are using the concept of normal as ideal (from their perspective).

3) *Normal as healthy.* Using the example above, some people may think that masturbation for young boys is not healthy. We often think of health and normal synonymously. If a person has a cancer in his lung, he is not thought of as normal in one sense. At least he doesn't have a normal lung, and if he has heart disease, he doesn't have a normal heart. He isn't normal. If a person is schizophrenic and hears voices that tell him to hurt people, he isn't normal. He has an abnormality in his brain. For these examples, "healthy" is equated with normal.

4) *Normal as process or development.* If a two year old has an accident and wets his pants, that is considered normal by most people. If a sixteen year old has an accident and wets his pants, that is considered a bit unusual, and probably as abnormal. It is developmentally normal for the two year old to have such an accident, but a sixteen year old usually has his sphincter under better control. Thus, what may be perfectly normal for one individual is not for another, depending on his or her developmental level. If a 39 year old man stands primping for hours in front of a mirror, it is seen differently than a 13 year old girl doing the same thing.

If nothing else comes from the comments above, it should be clear that the notion of "normal" is open to a variety of interpretations. As parents, we need to approach the value judgments that usually are associated with the designation "abnormal" very cautiously. Any consideration of normal should be utilized only to further the best interests of the child being evaluated, to lead to increased helpful attention, understanding and assistance.

Physical Development

In this discussion of development, let's start with *physical* development. It is more visible, more easily described, and its impact upon your child is sometimes more obvious than psychological or emotional development. From the time your baby is born, people are measuring your boy or girl's height and weight—from around twenty-two inches to five or six feet tall; from around seven pounds to one hundred to two hundred pounds of weight. This growth is pretty much over by the time they reach age twenty, but it is not a steady or an even process. Physical growth during childhood and adolescence usually has three distinct "spurts". The first one begins before birth and slows down during the first year of life. The second one covers ages two to seven, peaking around six or seven. The third one, the "adolescent growth spurt" begins very slowly around age seven or eight and reaches a peak around twelve for girls and fourteen for boys. Look at your teenagers and their classmates and you'll see that these are just averages. Adolescents vary remarkably as to the beginning, duration, and ending of their growth spurt. Sheer physical size affects a teenager's life in many ways—from what kinds of chores you give them to do, to what sports and recreation they enjoy, to what their status is in school, to when they begin actively seeking contact with the opposite sex, and so on.

As the body of your teenager grows, it is important to remember that all his or her parts are not growing at an even rate. Many adults see adolescents as "all hands and feet" and for a brief time the observation has basis in fact. During the adolescent growth spurt the extremes of the limbs reach peak size first, the foot before the calf and the calf before the thigh. In fact, after the head, your child's feet are the first part of the skeletal structure to stop growing. In the torso, hip width and chest size are reached several months before shoulder width. All this unevenness of growth is obvious to both adults and to the growing teenager, and to their friends, and it can become a source of embarrassment—"the awkward, ugly and repulsive age". The look of unevenness and lack of coordination that occurs at this time may be how the visual idea of "not being able to walk and chew gum at the same time" got started.

During the adolescent growth spurt the external and internal parts of the reproductive system grow spectacularly—a phenomenon generally labeled as "reaching puberty". There are two general kinds of changes that are going on. The first changes occur when the *primary sex characteristics* (the genitals and the internal reproductive parts) undergo enlargement and major structural changes. At the same time there are striking body modifications, called *secondary sex characteristics*, occurring; these are only indirectly associated with reproduction, but account for the most conspicuous differences between the sexes at adult ages. Your teenager is acutely aware of these changes and they affect his or her personality and behavior in many ways.

The first two secondary sex characteristics for both boys and girls are pubic hair and armpit hair (in that order, perhaps two years apart). The appearance of armpit hair usually occurs right around the peak of the growth spurt. At the same time, for boys, the sweat glands in the armpits enlarge (with increased sweating), and facial hair begins to grow above the upper lip. Also for boys, heavier hair begins to grow on the legs and forearms, and later appears on the upper arms and chest. During the second half of this growth spurt, the muscles of the larynx increase in size and the voice lowers. For girls, the two most obvious changes are the development of breasts (a process that takes two or three years) and the appearance of menstruation.

As was the case for height and weight, there is a lot of variation in timing for these signs of puberty—kids mature at different rates. Just visit a seventh grade class at the nearest school and you will see that the range is remarkable. You will find boys singing all the way from bass to soprano, yet they are within a few months of being the same age. You will see some girls with figures like a Playboy foldout and others who appear to have not yet begun to develop. Again, all these changes have far-reaching effects on behavior and personality. We saw a fourteen year old girl at the office a few years ago whose parents reported that she had been chronically depressed for the past six or eight months, refusing to go to school, saying she was ugly and nobody liked her. It only took a few minutes to discover that one notable part of her problem was a sister who was two years younger and was an *"early maturer"*. Her sister was, in the fourteen year old's words, "really built", tall, and "already a woman" (meaning to the older sister that she menstruated)—and the younger sister was regularly mistaken for the older of the two girls. To make matters worse, boys in the same grade as the fourteen year old were seeking her sister's attention and not hers. She had pretty well convinced herself that since she was older she had achieved all the physical development that she would ever get. Some understanding of the growth process laced with a little patience helped this young woman through a potentially serious emotional situation.

Generally speaking, early maturation provides a social and psychological advantage for children, and late development puts them at a disadvantage. The model that teenagers carry around for the ideal person is the "completed product", the adult. The development of breasts, lowering of the voice and enlarged muscles, are visible signs of "accomplishment" and looked at with envy by those not yet arrived. The early maturers are looked up to and treated as if "older and wiser". The very late maturer becomes self-conscious of her flat chest or his high voice. They are responded to more as "little kids", by peers and by adults. Additionally their participation and prowess in age-grouped sports and recreation may be limited. Enthusiasm for sports is imprinted at an early age and a few experiences of domination by early and "normal" age maturers with their larger muscles and greater endurance may turn an individual from physical competition for an extended time—perhaps even for life.

Psychological And Emotional Development

We've talked thus far about only one aspect of adolescent growth and development, the physical part. At the same time that the body is involved in change, so is the mind, or "psyche". It is very important to understand the highlights of psychological and emotional development. While a description of physical development is pretty cut and dried, the development of the mind can be approached from several viewpoints and at times can be tough to define. The psychological aspects of development include intelligence, relationship to the social world ("psychosocial"), conscience, and one's self-image. In each of these areas there are predictable stages of growth or change that generally occur, usually at certain ages, just like we encountered for physical development.

Temperament

Before talking about specific aspects of psychological and emotional development there are some general notions around the issue of genetically determined "temperament" that you should bear in mind. Have you, as a parent, ever been heard to say "he's always been that way ever since he was a baby?" You could be referring to any of a large number of personal traits (like stinginess, friendliness, perfectionism, sloppiness, or need for attention). Often parents comment on how different two of their kids are, and "always have been". "Darrell is very outgoing and never met a stranger he didn't like" while "Jason doesn't approach people; he needs some time to get to know". "Janet loves to play outside with the neighbor girls" while "Trisha usually spends her time inside watching television and playing with her dolls".

We all have some individual traits, some little quirks, that are as much a part of us as the color of our hair. They may be very pleasant parts of our personality or they may be irksome. For example, they may tend to make us very relaxed and easy-going, or to the contrary, we may be seen as an anxious and frantic kind of person. Our basic personality and social traits add up to temperament, something we probably are born with as the combination of factors that makes each of us uniquely individual. This temperament of ours also impacts on our surroundings and has an effect on how people react to us, and thus, on how we see the world.

Psychologists and philosophers have been arguing for centuries whether it is the genes we are born with or the environment we live in that determines personality—the *"nature versus nurture"* or *"heredity versus environment"* controversy. Were Darrell and Jason and Janet and Trisha, in the example above, born with those very different personality traits, or have they had some different life experiences that created them? Probably the best approach to this age-old question is to presume that personality is the result of both. Our biology gives us the basic temperament, the seeds of which are often *visible* in very young infants, but the environment makes a tremendous impact on the adult expression of that temperament. For example, the basic trait of perfectionism in one environment may express itself in neurotic, self-defeating and generally non-productive worrying. The same trait in interaction with a different environment may result in a psychologically healthy form of high achievement (like good grades in school or good job performance). As we talk below about specific aspects of psychological and emotional development, always bear in mind that progression through the various stages may be markedly affected by nature and nurture—by the basic temperament your child was born with and the experiences he has had since birth.

Intellectual Development

Intellectual development is very easy to see during childhood. At first there appears to be little or none, but very soon it is apparent that the child is able to learn things. The longer he or she exists in the environment, the better the child seems to be able to deal with it—from screaming at the top of his lungs when hungry, to asking for food, to opening the cupboard and raiding the cookie jar. The intellect brings orderliness and predictability to human behavior. In the beginning when your baby is hungry, with very limited brain ability, it can only scream, wiggle, fret and cry—innate reactions to physical discomfort. In stark contrast, the hungry adult carries out a purposeful series of actions to achieve the goal of obtaining nourishment. The development of intelligence results from simultaneous growth of the neurological system (brain, senses, and so on), increased interaction with the environment, and getting feedback from others.

Generally speaking, intellectual development is a continuous, slow-moving process with the most pronounced growth in the first fifteen or sixteen years of life. Thinking of it in stages, although somewhat arbitrary, will help you to differentiate the way children think from the way teenagers think from the way adults think. Jean Piaget spent most of his adult life studying intellectual development—from his work we can find four major stages of growth in young people. The first stage is called the *"sensorimotor state"*. The newborn infant doesn't "know" anything, it simply reacts, exercising innate reflexes. When presented with a nipple, the newborn doesn't know that putting its mouth over it and sucking will provide relief for internal discomfort (a "feeling" later he will learn to identify as hunger). The baby just starts sucking. During Piaget's first stage, pretty much the first two years of life, the child moves from reacting to things to knowing things. In his mind he begins to connect the present with the past and the future—he learned to climb up in his high chair when he was hungry, to go and get his blanket when he wanted to be put to bed, and that the upper right knob on the radio makes the music come on which brings his mother rushing into his room.

From ages two to around seven, children progress into Piaget's second stage, the *"preoperational stage"*. The most important thing about this stage is the conquest of symbols. During these years the child acquires language; his mind becomes able to deal with symbols. To see the difference in symbol use in these first two stages, offer a one-year-old and a six-year-old a five-dollar bill. The younger child may put the money in his mouth, tear it up, or ignore it, no matter how long you spend explaining its value. The six-year-old will probably be excited and ask the nearest adult to take him to the store, and he or she knows the result of that trip will be pleasant.

The *"concrete operations stage"*, from approximately ages eight to eleven, brings with it the ability to number, classify, order, and perform other feats of logic short of abstracting or theorizing. The child is bound by his or her view of reality but learns to logically organize it rather well. Offer a five-year-old and a ten-year-old a choice of either a dozen small pieces of candy or five much larger pieces. The five-year-old will probably opt for the larger quantity, while the older child figures out that he will end up with more by taking the smaller number of larger pieces. Or, take the two to a party where there is a magician performing. The younger one is more likely to be enthralled by the concept of "magic" and mystery and the power of adults. The ten-year-old is more likely to be the one to "blow the whistle" on the magician—he watches each ruse with studied preoccupation to determine the order and sequence of events in order to analyze the trick.

The fourth and final stage of Piaget's scheme of intellectual development is labeled *"formal operations"* and is the stage that applies to teenagers. It begins around age twelve and is nearly complete by age fifteen or sixteen. As a parent, you must have noticed how easy it was to outsmart your kids when they were little. When they were small you could give an order and they generally did what they were told, if they understood what you wanted and you looked serious. Then came those years when they would ask "Why?", and the older they got, the better your answers had to be. It's when they reach this fourth stage that many parents have the most difficulty with their kids. A child whose intellect has reached formal operations is no longer bound by his immediate experience. He or she not only can think about objects, but can think about thinking. Your child now can theorize, hypothesize, contemplate, and scrutinize. Youths at this age are typically beginning to come alive with "new" concepts. They may be bursting with enthusiasm about an English instructor who is teaching them about beauty, peace, or death. They may be marching or demonstrating about civil rights or capital punishment. They may be very concerned about the concepts of fairness or justice or war. Now when you explain "why?" to your child, he or she is able to evaluate abstractly the validity of your answers, or in teenage reality, argue much more effectively. The child may have argued at an earlier age, but you always had the upper hand—his rudimentary logic did not have a chance against your ability to abstract. Now sometimes the child's argument sounds good, not only to him, but to you, and that can be threatening. For example, you may have been relatively successful for years at keeping your preadolescent routinely doing his homework by telling him that he had to and that "all good boys and girls get good grades". Now that he can abstract, you may hear logical or near-logical arguments in many forms such as "I don't need to do anything but just pass, because I'm not going to college anyway" or "the other kids say he (the teacher) doesn't count the homework on your final grade" or "I prefer to do it just before the test so it will be fresh in my mind" or "don't hassle me all the time about it, I have the right to succeed or fail as I choose."

Successful intellectual development, that is, reaching Piaget's formal operations stage, effectively brings your child up to an adult level of functioning, though not an adult level of experience, preparing him and her to make their own way in this world. Successful parenting requires modifications in the ways in which you approach your child, depending upon where they are in the process. And you should be pleased if your child reaches your level of intellectual development (fourth stage)—even if their markedly improved debating skills are sometimes annoying!

Social Adaptation

Having looked at the issues of temperament and intellect, if you will use them as a background for what follows, we can go on to address the psychological and emotional development of your children from several different viewpoints. One of the most famous of approaches in this area was that of Erik Erikson—he proposed stages of human development that call attention to issues of social adaptation. As any of us grows up, we face a widening of our range of human relationships. Starting with just mom, then mom and dad, we ultimately must deal with the "world". According to Erikson, there are eight "psychosocial stages", five of which occur before adulthood. For each of these stages we must solve a specific set of "problems". Each stage has as one of the two alternative outcomes a very positive "resolution", such as trust or identity. There is also the possibility of incomplete resolution, a negative result, such as mistrust or role confusion. The solving of each stage's issues lays the groundwork for one part or one layer of the adult personality and enables us to move on to the next stage. Parents who have at least a rudimentary grasp of Erikson's first five psychosocial stages will find it much easier to understand their children, especially some of the peculiar fantasy or conformity or rebellion behaviors of young adolescents.

During the first year of our life, we begin with the stage called *trust vs. mistrust*. If our needs are attended to fully and dependably, the world is seen as "good", stable and safe—a place to be trusted—and according to Erikson that view will likely stay with us throughout our lives. Generally, during our infancy a stable personality characteristic is created, one that will forecast how we will deal with people on through adulthood. We will usually approach other people in a very trusting manner, or in a very distrustful way, or in some predictable place between these two extremes. However, the learning of trust or distrust (or any of the issues from Erikson's eight stages) are not absolute or final, and can be modified in either direction by later events. The more impactful (pleasant or traumatic) the event, the more the likelihood of altering an individual's early resolution of the trust vs. mistrust stage (or other stages). Psychotherapy or counseling is often called upon to help provide some movement when individuals are impeded in life by a negative stage result (for example, they are regularly mistrustful of everyone around them). In our many years of practice we have encountered numerous teenagers whose lives are made miserable or difficult because of their lack of progression through early social developmental stages. It's tough to go through life filled with shame and doubt or mistrusting all adults or feeling inferior to your peers.

During the second year of life, we encounter the stage of *autonomy vs. shame and doubt*. The toddler is becoming aware of himself as a person among other people, and wants to take care of things without adult help. He demonstrates the drive for autonomy or self-direction in many and varied ways (earning the nickname of the "terrible twos" for this stage)—in mastery of his own body (walking, climbing, jumping, and so on), in mastery of objects (carrying things, opening things, putting on clothing, and so on), and in social relationships (learning language, refusing to do what you ask, hitting other children, and so on). The push to autonomy is by no means absolute and unrelenting (watch them run to mommy if frightened or confused), but is always evident. The opposite of autonomy developmentally is shame and self-doubt which occurs if a certain amount of self-direction is not allowed or encouraged by the parents. Such a child may learn to feel "bad", vulnerable and impotent, rather than confident and capable of autonomy or self-direction.

During the third, fourth and fifth years, children move to what in many respects is a refinement and elaboration of the previous stage—to the stage called *initiative vs. guilt*. If parents and other adults routinely squelch the child's initiative (his or her goal-directed, purposefully planned activities), the resulting effect of all that negative feedback is feelings of guilt around such normal developmental activities. For example, if a four-year-old brings his mother a picture he has drawn looking for her approval, she may make some positive comments about the unintelligible lines, or she may put the kid off. If she gives him praise, he is more likely to continue to pursue drawing and other similar tasks. If she gives him a message of discouragement (either directly by negative comment, or indirectly by lack of any response), he is more likely to think something is wrong with it (and maybe also with him) and be less inclined to pursue it, maybe even feeling guilty about what he has done, because it was obviously not pleasing to mom. Children need affirmation. The following true story illustrates this point. A young child, playing by himself, stopped and asked his mother to join him. The mother told him she was busy and couldn't stop to play now. The child said, "Oh, you don't need to play with me; just watch me and say, 'wonderful, wonderful.'"

From the end of the initiative vs. guilt stage to the onset of puberty is stage four, *industry vs. inferiority*, a further elaboration of the previous two stages. Successfully dealing with the issues of this stage leaves the child with a sense of competence. He is inclined to do things and feels he will be able to do them well! Lack of positive resolution here is seen in pervasive and generalized feelings of inferiority.

Have you ever heard the expression "identity crisis"? It is often applied to teenagers. For Erikson, the fifth stage is for the teenage years and is called *identity vs. role confusion*. It begins with the onset of puberty and continues for four to seven years. During this period of life the teenager must define who he or she is—and this simple sounding task is full of pitfalls. Your child is faced with the problem of making sense out of his entire past, selecting who and what he would like to be in the future, and somehow deal with all this, and with reality, in the present. The past can hang people up, especially when it is a whole lot different than what the person would like it to be. The future is complex, and sometimes frightening with more options than anyone can imagine. And all these options have to be sorted. Also, current reality always impinges on defining our identities—some definitions just won't wash, they are just fantasy. Watch your teenagers as they struggle with identity. Psychologically healthy teens will be constantly sorting through all the information they can muster, with special attention to the feedback they get from their peers. Periodically they've "got it all together" or are at loose ends, they are down on themselves or are inflated with pride, they can realistically evaluate their abilities or are "living a dream", they show a realistic and "mature" focus for the future or are wallowing in indecision. Over the years, a common motivation that brings teenagers into our office to talk to us (without their parents dragging them in) is to get feedback from a "professional" as to who they are, looking to better understand their developing adult personality. When identity issues involve educational and vocational planning, they often seek out school counselors to get some clarity on these kinds of issues. Very important as identity "guides" are the adolescent's parents. Typical progression through this stage involves a lot of "checking" with significant others in the teenager's world and the parents are usually a very safe place to begin. How many times have your youngsters asked questions like "am I beautiful", "am I hard to get along with", "would I make a good teacher", "do I have a good singing voice", "should I try out for soccer", "how do you think I would do on the debate team", and so on. Your answers to these questions help your child to more clearly define his or her identity.

If your children make it through the identity vs. role confusion stage successfully, they will have a sense of understanding themselves, a sense of wholeness, a sense of belonging, and a sense of purpose to their lives. They will know who they are and where they are going—and that is what identity is. Also, very importantly, they have become ready to proceed to Erikson's next stage—*intimacy vs. isolation.* Successful resolution here is a prerequisite for close and lasting adult-to-adult interpersonal relationships.

For some parents, their older teenagers will begin to approach, and perhaps enter, Erikson's stage of intimacy. The earlier teen years are spent with the kids focusing a great deal on peer norms—what the guys or girls are doing, saying, wearing, or thinking. This helps kids to get a sense of themselves in comparison to their peer group. As they get older and more sure of themselves, and as they are more clear about their own personal values and likes and dislikes, they have more flexibility to strike out on their own, away from groups, and pair off with other individuals who share their interests and values. There is often a long string of "romantic" pairings in late adolescence, offering the teenager many trials at how to form friendships with and how to be emotionally close to the opposite sex, or sometimes to the same sex. Experiencing many different, relatively short-term relationships, a youngster is setting the stage for the development of longer lasting intimate relationships to come into his or her adult life. Those teenagers who do not experience these bonds (through fear and avoidance, restrictive parents, or locking into one very early relationship for an excessive amount of time) miss out on a very valuable set of experiences in forming relationships. Typical adolescent pairings offer encounters with a gamut of behaviors and emotions including giving, humor, sharing, conflict, and loving—a wonderful preparation for the pleasures and pains of adulthood. Think of all your youngster's relationships, both with males and females, as "practicing". And practice makes perfect, that is, practice should lead to successful and rewarding friendships in adulthood.

Moral Development
A crucial concern for most parents is that their children develop a good *conscience.* They want them to grow up with inter-

nal controls, a set of personal limits that assure socially accept- able behavior. Everyone has read in the newspapers about people who commit horrible, brutal crimes, and most people reflecting on them wonder "how he or she could ever do something like that." You may wonder if the criminal feels badly about it, what kind of upbringing he had, whether he is crazy, if he went to church, and so on. Part of growing up is learning what is so- cially acceptable behavior and what is not. It begins at a very young age—remember, "Good boy!" when little Joey helped his daddy stack wood or *"No, naughty*!" when Jennifer stomped on the puppy's tail. Through these simple kinds of comments, you were beginning the process of helping your child to build inter- nal controls. Successful internal controls will allow him to avoid running afoul of the law, to feel good about himself, and to es- tablish lasting and intimate interpersonal relationships. Con- science is, however, a very complex aspect of one's personality and comes in several different forms.

Louis Kohlberg has defined six stages of conscience develop- ment (or "morality"), and he refers to progression through these stages as "moral development". The first, called *"punishment and obedience"*, describes the morality of the toddler through age five or six. Goodness or badness of an action is totally determined by its physical consequences. The child will avoid a certain behav- ior not because it is personally or morally or socially disagree- able, but because he gets a swat on the fanny (or "time out" or yelled at or some other distasteful "feedback" from others)—he yields to physical power, to direct punishment. The inverse is also true; his or her behaviors which bring smiles, pats, treats and other rewards, tend to be repeated and are defined by the toddler as "good". Thankfully, as we discussed above, intellectu- al development is rapid through the first few years of life. Thus, your toddler very rapidly learns what behaviors you demand that they stop and what behaviors will please you and should be repeated.

During ages five or six to eleven or twelve, the child's ap- proach to morality is expanded into stage two, *"selfish sharing"*. During this stage the notions of fairness and sharing become fixed in the child's conscience, but always interpreted in a selfish, physical, and practical way—"You scratch my back and I'll scratch yours." Sharing occurs only when the child's needs are also met and not because of principles like gratitude, loyalty, or justice. Watch a group of eight-year-olds at play and you will see moments of helpfulness, fairness and sharing, but also watch how quickly they vanish when the sharer is no longer amused by or interested in the interaction.

Most children during early adolescence (starting around age eleven or twelve) are in stage three of conscience development, *"pleasing others"*. At this stage, behavior is no longer completely dependent upon the child's own selfish needs. He or she begins to define good behavior as that which pleases or helps others. Generally, these kids of middle school age still respond to the significant adults in their life, but are also remarkably influenced by their peers. They regularly form cliques and groups and gangs, and the kids they hang out with as well as others in their life space all can be important for this stage. The typical child becomes a "conformist" to society's expectations, is loyal to it, and works hard to maintain it. During this stage the child gains the ability to judge behavior by intention rather than consequences—"he means well" or "he didn't mean to cause a problem." A lot of parents mistake this stage for adult (level five or six) morality. Outwardly, you may behave morally in essentially the same way as your child, although probably conforming less rigidly, both verbally and in the trappings (clothes, hair styles, and so on). However, it is a mistake to presume your thirteen-year-old can give anything but lip service to the complex ethical principles that guide most adults, concepts like "equality", "human rights", and "brotherly love." For this child, simply put, "being nice" pleases others and generates approval; no more, no less. For parents, it is always pleasing when a child reaches this stage—after years of "selfishness", it is great to see him become "other-directed". You may see the abandonment of behaviors that have annoyed you for years, simply because he now so actively avoids disapproval, especially from his peers. You may have harped on it for years to no avail, but when his buddies make fun of him once, he changes his ways!

Kids in their middle teens usually move into stage four of conscience development —*"law and order"*. During this stage, the concept of "duty" becomes important. Good behavior consists of "doing one's duty", respecting authority and preserving fixed rules and the social order for their own sake. "Everyone will be happy if they just follow all the rules", and "we need laws because without them, people will be fighting all the time" characterizes the thinking of the typical middle teen. This kind of morality represents their conscience and routinely guides their behavior. Adults often find kids in this stage overly rigid, and get frustrated because they don't seem to see past rules and laws to guiding principles—hence, they don't really independently evaluate what is going on. They tend to react argumentatively to the letter of the law (and often to look for loopholes in the law as it applies to them).

Sometime during the middle to late teens, most people take the last steps in conscience development, moving to stages five and six (which are very close to the same, so we'll treat them as one). We'll call this last stage *"moral values and principles"*. The teenager's conscience begins to take the form of generalized moral values and ethical principles (for example, "The Golden Rule") that they have chosen as important and good and not strictly the rules and laws that have been set down by others for them to follow (for example, "The Ten Commandments). Now we see the application of universal abstract notions like, "justice", "human rights", and the "sacredness of life". Your child's behavior becomes directed by these principles and his or her interpretation of their application to their own lives. For a lot of late teens and young adults, much energy is devoted to grasping, sorting, and making "practical sense" out of these complex principles, and as they do, many become annoyed (or even enraged) at the existence of situations to the contrary. Adding these newfound moral principles and the increasing understanding of the use of these principles to the enthusiasm and energy of young people, we can understand a lot of "youth movements" in our society—"peace and love" themes, cult groups with their communes and slogans like "one for all and all for one", peace marchers in their battle against war, candlelight vigils against the death penalty, protests against cutting forests, sit-ins against racial or other discrimination, rallies against abortion, and so on.

Parents are regularly concerned about their children's behavior, aware when it is good and very aware when it is not good. The bad behaviors like lying, stealing, disobedience, and the like, bring more families into our offices than do obvious emotional problems (like severe depression or anxiety). It is important for parents to understand the nature of their child's conceptualization of good and bad, that is, his conscience. With that knowledge, they have a better chance at dealing with what they see as "bad behavior".

Self-Concept

Another approach to describing psychological and emotional development, and the last we will present, deals with "self concept". You will see as we define it, it shares some similarities with the concept of identity that we discussed earlier. Everyone has some notion as to what they are like as a person, their good points and their bad points, and bear in mind, we all have both. We say if someone generally likes what they see, they have "good self-esteem". If they don't think much of themselves, we would say they have "poor self-esteem". We regularly see teenagers (and adults) in our offices who are seriously critical of themselves. The extreme of this is someone who hates himself or certain things about himself so much that he acts it out by attempting suicide. A basic proposition of life on this planet is that everyone wants to be happy and to be happy you have to feel okay about yourself. Self concept is very important, so we'll explain what it is and where it comes from.

When your child was born, he had no ideas about anything, including himself. In fact, it takes several weeks before a baby can distinguish between his body and objects around him, and he certainly is not ready to mentally conceive of and evaluate himself as a person. Think of the baby's self concept as a book with all the pages blank—they will be filled in over the years. Until about age five or six, the self-concept is very simple and very general, like "good girl" or "bad girl", and very unstable (it can change radically in seconds). During this time the self-concept essentially mirrors the comments and actions of others directed toward the child – the "looking glass self". The child measures himself purely by the responses of others to his behavior—he *is* what he is told. He has good self-esteem or poor self-esteem depending upon how close he lives up to the expectations of the people around him, and in the early years, the "others" with most of the impact are you, his parents.

During the next few years (ages six to twelve) the child's views of himself take on some stability—and by the end of this time period, they are more tenacious than most people realize. We saw an eleven-year-old boy in the office recently whose parents described him as depressed, lazy, and as having a terrible self-image. When interviewed, his feelings about himself were much like those the parents had described—"I can't do anything", "the other kids don't like me", "I'm dumb", and "I hate myself" were all uttered during that first session. In a later meeting we found out that his grades in school were excellent (almost all A's), that when he tried sports he always excelled, and that just about everybody around him liked him. He apparently had developed a poor self image at a very young age and large amounts of ordinary feedback to the contrary at age eleven did little to affect it. His self concept was remarkably "crystallized".

We frequently see people in our office who have made decisions about themselves as children, with the age-appropriate thinking of children at the ages the decisions were made, who continue to hang on to these decisions into their adult lives. Unless these decisions are revisited and re-examined and evaluated in the light of later developmental stages, they can continue to hamper individuals for life. A good example of this was the child whose teacher in the second grade was very critical of his art work. The child decided at that time that he just was not a good artist. From that point on he refused to really try his best at art work and avoided it whenever he could. Fortunately, in his sophomore year of high school, he had a biology teacher who required hand-drawn copies of drawings from the textbook to go into a notebook. These were essential to a good grade in the class. Having an avid interest in science, the student dutifully worked at the drawings, and surprisingly to him, the drawings turned out looking much like the ones in the book. Through this experience he surmised that perhaps he had been mistaken, that he wasn't such a bad artist after all—but it took him about ten years to serendipitously find that out. He re-examined his previous decision in light of new data. Many people don't have the opportunity to do that unless they consciously work at it, or someone leads them to it.

Through those same years that the self-concept becomes stable, another factor comes into play—the child begins to develop goals for himself as a person. He will want to be "macho" or smart or friendly or whatever. Often the child cannot express these specific kinds of goals directly as can older teenagers, but they are expressed in the form of fantasy or play or "what I want to be when I grow up". The main impact of developing goals for your child is that now he has another yardstick, an internal one, against which to measure his self-concept. For years he compared his views of himself with what others said about him and if there wasn't much discrepancy, he was happy. Now he will continue doing that, but also he will compare his self conception with goals he sets for himself, goals which he will elaborate and refine at a rapid rate over the next several years.

People, and your teenager is no exception, constantly evaluate their own behavior and that evaluation impacts upon their concept of self. The evaluation is really twofold—looked at in light of how it impacts on others and reflected back by them, and how it stacks up against the goals and ideals the person has for himself. Thinking of these mechanisms helps parents to better understand some of their teenager's behavior. For example, many kids have an overwhelming need to conform—"Dad, all the other kids are wearing them" or "everyone else is learning to play tennis". Through conformity they don't risk negative feedback from their peers. Prolonged criticism at school will shake their self-esteem, whereas regular acceptance is supportive of many positive aspects of their self-concept. The need we all have for accepting one's self is why "peer pressure" is so powerful. Most adults are not affected as dramatically by social pressure, because their concepts of self are much more stable or "crystallized". We say "most" adults because all mental health professionals have encountered very socially dependent adults—often the problems their dependency creates bring them to seek counseling. The self-concept was born from the reactions of others. After several years it began to be affected by personal goals. In adulthood the emphasis should switch more and more to internal direction from one's goals and ideals, and most of us lose any emphasis or strong dependency upon feedback from others—"he's his own man".

For the rest of this book we will talk about specific areas which often concern parents trying to live through their kids' teen years. In doing so, we will discuss many specific problems which most of us face with our kids at one time or another, and we will try to give you some indication of what's going on to give you some hints on how to handle it, but all of that information must be interpreted in light of the child's development. You handle a thirteen-year-old's drug problem differently than an eighteen-year-old's. You can ignore the fact that your thirteen-year-old thinks war would be fun, but the eighteen-year-old should not be so positive about it. You handle a thirteen-year-old's desire to own a horse differently than an eighteen-year-old's. You will help a thirteen-year-old to organize his homework to make sure he gets it all done; an eighteen-year-old should be able to handle it independently. Through the teenage years your child is in the process of "growing up", physically and psychologically—in the beginning of this stage of life he is a child, and at the end of it he is an adult. As a parent you must change your perceptions, expectations, and interactions as he grows up.

Development itself can be a tremendous problem. We've already pointed out that late physical maturation can create social difficulties for your child. Incomplete or very late psychological and emotional development can present even bigger crises. The majority of kids will progress through the various stages we have outlined pretty much on time and in sync with their peers, but consider the added problems in growing up for the older teenager who cannot think abstractly, or the very dependent early teen who has not yet learned initiative, or the selfish adolescent who is stuck at stage two in conscience development, or the teenager who finds his goals and ideals way out of reach or that others are not accepting of them. As mental health professionals we mostly see the kids who are out of step, the teens who for one reason or another are stuck or way behind developmentally. If we are going to stimulate growth, we need to remember that these kids initially need to be dealt with at their current level of development, not where their development "should" be. They are the kids who are extremely immature or very depressed or highly anxious or always angry or regularly obstinate or even very crazy. We will talk more about these most problematic teenagers in a later part of this book. For now, remember that all kids are sometimes a little immature or briefly depressed or somewhat tense or occasionally obstinate, and as parents, you need to deal with those problems. Most of this book is for those ordinary kids, and for their sometimes frustrated and confused parents who are working hard just to stay one jump ahead of their offspring. If we are lucky, we may be able to say one day, "Why is it that about the time they get civilized, they leave?"

Pearls For Parents:

1) Remember that children vary in their development, that there is no rigid timetable. Each child in a family will be different in various aspects. Intellectual ability, emotional maturity, physical stature, and conscience will not all develop at some magic "correct" day for each kid. Just as a child's feet grow large before his muscles fill out his chest and back, so will other aspects of his development occur unevenly in spurts at different times as he matures. You should think of nature as filling in the pieces as they become available, sort of like hunting and gathering, and not like putting together a Chevy truck on an assembly line.

2) Parents are and always have been the primary source of feedback for youngsters in all areas of psychological, emotional and social growth. Be alert to when your child is in a "learning mode" on any issue of development and jump in with the best information and/or affirmation that you can muster.

3) There are stages in a kid's life that are not fun, not pretty, not easy, but they have to go through them and so do we. Try to be patient with the unesthetic, the dumb, and the thoughtless. They have to learn through their mistakes, just as we did (and still do). Try to show them how to deal with their mistakes by showing them how we deal with ours.

4) Remember that kids make decisions about themselves that are age-appropriate at the time, but when held onto into later years, become burdensome and erroneous. Try to give them opportunities to re-examine those decisions and ideas in the light of their advanced development.

Books

Childhood and Society by Erik Erikson
W.W.Norton and Co., Inc., New York, 1950, 1963

The Construction of Reality in the Child by Jean Piaget
Basic Books, New York, 1954

The Child's Conception of the World by Jean Piaget
Humanities Press, New York, 1951

The Origins of Intelligence in Children by Piaget
International University Press, New York, 1952

Child Psychology 62nd Yearbook of the National Society
   for the Study of Education edited by H.W.Stevenson
"Moral Development and Identification"
   by Lewis Kohlberg University of Chicago Press, Chicago, 1963
Temperament and Development by Alexander Thomas and Stella Brunner/Mazel Publishers, New York,
   1977 Chess Reviving Ophelia by Mary Pipher Ph.D.
(about adolescent girls) Ballantine Books, New York 1995

The Magic Years by Selma Fraiberg
(about early childhood development)
May be out of print—look in used book stores.

Making Sense of Adolescence—How to Parent From The Heart
by John Crudele, C.S.P. and Richard Erickson Ph.D.
Triumph Books
Liquore, Missouri 1995

<u>Parenting Teens With Love and Logic</u>
by Foster Cline, M.D. and Jim Fay
Pinon Press
P.O. Box 35007, Colorado Springs, CO 80935
1992

Classic Movies:
"Rambling Rose" (Laura Dern, Robert Duvall)
"The Summer of '42" (Jennifer O'Neill)
"The Sterile Cuckoo" (Liza Minnelli)
"The Outsiders" (Matt Dillon)
"The Flamingo Kid" (Richard Crenna, Matt Dillon)
"My Bodyguard" (Matt Dillon)
"A Bronx Tale" (DeNiro, Palmieri)
"Big" (Tom Hanks)
"The Boy With Green Hair" (Dean Stockwell—child actor — Robert Ryan, Barbara Hale, Pat O'Brien)
"The Man Without A Face" (Mel Gibson)
"The Breakfast Club" (Ally Sheedy, Molly Ringwald, Judd Nelson, Emilio Estevez, Anthony Michael Hall)
"Rebel Without a Cause" (James Dean, Natalie Wood)
"Footloose" (Kevin Bacon)
"Sixteen Candles" (Anthony Michael Hall, Molly Ringwald)
"Good Will Hunting" (Robin Williams, Matt Damon)
"Brooklyn"

Occasionally we may suggest a web site, but for the most part, people know how to google for more information, so unless we have a particularly useful site, we'll leave the googling up to you.

Chapter 3
COMMUNICATION

"All animals are equal but some animals
are more equal than others"
— **George Orwell ANIMAL FARM**

A few years back an elementary school teacher referred a young boy to our office for evaluation. I referred to this case in the first chapter. He had recently been presented with a new infant brother, and since his sibling's birth his drawings at school had begun to worry the teacher. Despite access to numerous colors the boy's drawings were done all in black—the teacher was concerned that this child was depressed as a result of the new addition to his family. The worried parents brought the child to us at the teacher's suggestion.

We greeted this youngster, and he seemed reasonably cheerful, and we got out crayons and paper. Sure enough, the first crayon he grabbed was the black one, and he proceeded to draw a landscape and a house all in black. We commented, "Boy, you sure seem to like black." His reply was, "I sure do; it's the same color as licorice and that's my favorite candy!" After spending the rest of the session with this child, we concluded there was no evidence that he was depressed; indeed, he actually felt pretty positive about his new little brother. It was just that *people around him jumped to conclusions and didn't stop to do a very simple but fundamental step in communicating with this youngster—ask him why he was coloring everything in black.* Although the incident described above occurred for a younger child, the same principle exists with teenagers. Some very complicated appearing "problems" can sometimes clear up rather quickly by simply asking straight questions, listening carefully, and getting straight answers.

A critical aspect of our role as parents is that of teacher. By the time your child reaches adolescence you have taught him or her an amazing amount of things. We need to help our kids learn, first and foremost, *how to survive,* and secondly, and not far behind, *how to love and to be intimate* with others. Human beings are social creatures by nature. Most adults actively seek pleasant, rewarding, relationships with others. We want the same for our offspring. In order to teach our kids the social skills necessary to establish and maintain relationships, we need to teach the basic building block, the most fundamental skill, *"communication".* Without it there can be no significant relationships. And with poor communication there will be difficult relationships. Effective communication is useful for surviving and for securing creature comforts, but its role in intimate interpersonal relationships is essential. As mental health professionals, a great deal of the work we do in the office with families and couples deals with communication—we cannot stress enough just how fundamental it is to human beings getting along with and enjoying one another!

All of us as parents have a whole storehouse of information that we can pull out of our hats when we are trying to figure out how to deal with our kids. We just have to think back and ask ourselves, "What did my father do in this kind of situation?" or "What would my mother have said now?" A lot of this kind of parenting information is useful. It was taught to us by our parents or other significant adults in our lives, either directly or through example. These are the social skills that we learned, about how to handle relationships, and most of us still struggle with them. In all the various kinds of parenting situations we must face over the course of several years of child rearing we cannot always be certain we are doing the "right" thing, partly because we are guessing, partly because our parents' teaching to us wasn't necessarily always clear, and partly because no two circumstances are exactly identical. Even if something was a good idea for them, it might not be for us in a new time and a little different situation with other people. One of the most important questions that you can ask yourself after wondering what your mother or father would have done in this kind of situation is, "Was their approach a good idea?" Most parents come to realize that their parents were winging it sometimes in this parenting thing just like we are.

The notions of "good idea" and "bad idea" have to be examined. Good idea/bad idea or good parenting/bad parenting are concepts that tend to carry moral value, and most attempts at parenting are not good or bad in a moral sense. Thankfully, most of us are trying to be good. We're also trying to be *"effective"* parents, and effective implies some sort of positive outcome. What is the end result? The implication here is that to be an effective parent, one has to be aiming for something, a definable product, and that some process has to take place to reach that desired end. The end result of effective parenting is that your kids will have learned how to survive and how to love and form intimate relationships. They aren't born with social skills. The process that must occur for that outcome is a learning process—your kids are students, and you parents are teachers.

Many people have looked at the job of parenting, especially the teaching part, and said to themselves, "Oh brother, how did I get into this? I didn't count on all this, and my kids are already teenagers. I don't know the first thing about teaching, and now I'm supposed to take it up as a career." Don't panic. You know a lot more than you think about teaching your kids. You have been doing it for years! All we are suggesting is that you give some thought as to how to do it most "effectively" (that word again). Classroom teachers, for example, start out with lesson plans. They decide what they want to teach, and they set up a structure and process that will help them to get through that material. We all remember and were impressed by the teachers who came prepared and knew their stuff. Parents are in a similar situation. It is uncomfortable for us and for our kids when we are uncertain. Kids as well as grownups like a certain amount of predictability and routine, so when we are clear about our thoughts and behaviors and decisions, our kids tend to be more comfortable and learn more. It is very important for this task of being an effective teacher to our kids to be able to sort out and clarify our own thinking about what it is that we want them to learn—then we have to look at how we can best communicate these things to them. If our goal is effective parenting, and that means effective teaching, obviously to teach we must be able to effectively communicate.

Issues of teaching aside, in order to maintain harmony and mutual satisfaction in any relationship, including one with your children, communication is essential. Over the next several pages we will present some general notions about communication, define several specific aspects of communication, talk about various communication skills, and give both theoretical and practical ideas we hope will be helpful.

Let's start out with some general discussion of what communication is all about. If we want to communicate with someone, we are saying we want to get some ideas or thoughts across to another person. We want that person to clearly understand what it is that we want him to know. That doesn't necessarily mean communicating everything we are thinking about (or wearing our hearts on our sleeve, so to speak), but just getting across those thoughts that we want the other person to understand. Thus, the first aspect of communication (and an extremely important one) that we will talk about is clarity. Is what we are saying clear or unclear?

Clarity

Let's look at a dialogue between a mother and her fifteen year old son after she has overheard part of a telephone conversation between her son and his friend:

Mother: "I heard you talking with your friend on the phone about a kegger last weekend and it sounded like you were making plans for something similar this weekend. You know that I don't approve of your drinking. Can you explain what is going on?"

Son: "What, are you doing listening in on my conversations?"

Mother: "I wasn't listening in. I happened to walk in while you were speaking on the phone and couldn't help but overhear part of the conversation. Please tell me what is going on."

Son: "You're always nosing into my business."

Mother: "I'm not going to get distracted by an argument about eavesdropping. I accidentally caught part of your conversation, but I'm glad that I did. I'm the parent and you're a minor. I am responsible for your safety and how your behavior impacts on the safety of others, so I still would like some explanation."

As you can see, mother attempted to present her issues clearly. The son knows what the issues are, and whatever he ends up choosing to do, he is going to know where his parent stands and why. Mother has made things clear so that if her son chooses to defy her, she can easily take the next step of consequating his behavior, that is, enact some form of "punishment". The son, in the meantime, also may be secretly relieved that he does not have to bow to peer pressure, and he now has mom as a "heavy" to blame if he does not want to show up at the kegger. It is important to remember that until kids mature, they will overtly tend to push the "system" (their parents included) for as much as they can get, but covertly they like to know where the limits are. Since they are somewhere midway in the process of developing internal controls, having no limits from parents scares kids. Until they have learned how to put the stops on for themselves, they need external limit-setters to do that for them, and they often feel relief and a sense of security when words are clarified and behavior is contained.

We have had numerous troubled, out of control teenagers tell us in the office that they envy those kids whose parents "care enough" to discipline and control them. You parents know it is one part of your job that takes a whole lot of effort, and it can create a lot of frustration for you. Some parents just give up, turning their children loose long before they are ready to function in the world on their own. These kids without significant external guidance are very often anxious and/or depressed as they try to get through life (school, peers, work or whatever) on their own. They feel like a ship without a home port, with no place to go for repairs and fuel. Keep on teaching and protecting your children well into their teenage years. Don't turn your kids completely loose from your apron strings until they are really ready! You and your child will know when that time is upon you.

To be an "effective" parent, during teenage developmental years you must gradually let go, more and more as time passes, but still keep monitoring, checking and being ready to contain if necessary. At the same time, parents need to be able to accept the fact that kids will make choices, and that these choices will not always be choices the parents would make. In order for your child to grow and mature toward independence, some of these have to be allowed in order for the youngster to gain a reservoir of experience from which he or she learns. This occasionally requires a lot of biting one's tongue, but hold onto a willingness to step in on important issues, and to provide very clear communication of your feelings and directives. Always step in when the potential for a disastrous outcome is there. When the possible outcomes are much less serious, let them learn through experience. Effective parents have an excellent sense of when to take over and when to let go, and regularly are evaluating situations from the perspective of what is best for their child (and not themselves).

Verbal Vs. Non-Verbal

Verbal communication is made up of words. This does not always mean that the words will be clear, nor does it mean that the words will always be factual or correct. Words can distort, words can lie and words can be confusing, but since most of our thoughts occur in language, using words seems to be the most efficient way to communicate to other human beings. Think about it—can you see anything in the room you are now in for which a word does not immediately come to mind? Chair, table, window, clock, paper, wall, and so on. We tend to think in language. We may occasionally have images in our minds of fishing alongside a quiet brook or of lying in a meadow watching clouds, but most of our thoughts occur like we were talking to ourselves. The language we use is very important to the way we think, including the way we think about ourselves.

Eskimos have many different words for snow. Snow is very important to them. It can be crystalline, fluffy, wet, dry, blowing, drifting, melting, and so on. Each form has a different word because snow is a major element in their lives, so they want to be very precise when talking about it. Years ago we read about a culture that had many, many different words for love. That group of people differentiates very clearly between the love of a husband and wife, of a teacher and student, of a brother and sister, of a father and son, between father and daughter, of lovers in a new and exciting romance, and so on. That particular culture has language that is much more precise than English in regards to love. The more precise we can be with language, the greater the potential for clear communication. Ponder, for example, the young man who says to the young woman, "I love you", when what he means is, "I am feeling aroused and want to have sex with you, and I sort of like you too." The woman, on the other hand, may be interpreting it to mean, "I am exhilarated by being with you, and I respect you as a person, and I want to be your best friend." These are definitely different messages that can be communicated by the same three words, "I love you."

Many parents get rattled when their kids say "I hate you", especially when they sound like they really mean it. It is important to recognize that "hate" is a word that does not have many suitable substitutes or variations in the English language. Some people feel it is the direct opposite of "love"—so if "love" means operating in another person's best interests forever (or for a long time at least), then hate must be wishing evil things on someone forever. They don't realize that kids who say, "I hate you!" are usually saying, "I am really angry at you right now and the strongest expression of my anger I can muster at the moment is to say I hate you." They forget that these same kids are dependent on them, that parents are the safest people on whom to express a lot of anger (because they represent "home" and one place that they can safely let down their social guards), and that a kid's sense of time and lasting effects of words are much different than that of adults. This same kid may be cheerfully asking "What's for dinner?" within the hour.

Despite the numerous inaccuracies and pitfalls that can occur for verbal communication, it has the potential for being a very powerful means to exchange ideas with another human being. Now that we've talked about verbal communication and indicated that it isn't always perfect, let's talk about communication of the *non-verbal* type. There is a school of thought that says when two or more people are together, there is no such thing as non-communication, that one cannot "not communicate". Take the example of the man who sits on a bus or plane next to another man. The second man immediately picks up his newspaper and begins to read it—one communication here is that he is "telling" the first man that he is not interested in conversation. If the story ended here, there still was communication. Next, despite the newspaper, imagine that the first man attempts to start up a conversation. The second man gives him short, one word answers, never looking up from his paper. Very soon the first man drops the conversation and opens up his magazine. Clearly a series of communications has occurred here, but not all of them used words. What is meant by non-verbal communication? Just what it says—it is communication that doesn't use words, like leaning toward someone as they talk to show interest, or looking away from someone as they talk to show irritation or disinterest. Men and women's courtship encounters are full of non-verbal "cues", messages from one person to the other that are not language based. Our society has tended to shy away from straight forward language when romance is involved, so a sensitivity to the non-verbal forms of "yes" and "no" is usually important as people court.

The term *body language* has been used to depict an approach for interpreting body posture, gait, facial expression, and so on, and to describe the meanings which these behaviors carry. Most of us are threatened if someone with clenched fists and tight lips steps right in front of us, only standing a foot or two away. Most of us are not threatened by someone with a smile on his face who sits down in a very relaxed, legs crossed position. We read the body language from the first guy as tense and aggressive and dominating. The body language of the second guy suggests he is not tense and is acquiescent. We all have learned to read these non-verbal body and face cues in any kind of human-to-human interactions.

The person who comes stiffly into our office, speaks rather coolly, sits on a chair way across the room, crosses his arms and legs, and asks, "Okay doctor, what can you tell me about my kid?", has already clearly told us that he is resistant to the idea of coming for help and is reluctant to open up to the idea of participating in counseling. The teenager who enters our office, clearly avoiding any physical contact with parents, sits with a sullen expression and refuses to speak, has said a great deal without moving his lips—for example, "I didn't want to come here" or "You think I'm crazy" or "My parents are creeps for getting me into this" or "You're going to be sorry you brought me here" or "I'm not going to talk and give this shrink anything to go on." On a positive note, we have had lots of youngsters who come into our office and assume an attentive, sit-on-the-edge of their chair posture, with a smiling face—body language which says "I'm open to listening to what this guy has to say, cause maybe it will help my situation".

In addition to what we could call "*T-shirt messages*", non-verbal expressions of feeling that are displayed openly like statements on T-shirts, there are many other kinds of behavior which are non-verbal, but nonetheless they still relay messages. Some of these can be very subtle. Examples of these types of non-verbal communications include distracting behaviors, forgetting, thoughtlessness, neglecting (things that don't get done that are supposed to), and doing or saying things that are known to set off predictable chain reactions.

All of us who are parents usually recognize when a youngster is coming onto the scene with a behavior that is *distracting*, usually in order to get some attention. This is much more easily recognized in a three-year-old than a sixteen-year-old, because it is usually done with more finesse and much more subtly by the older child. They no longer just jump into your lap while you are trying to oil your fishing reel or peel the potatoes. In either case there is a message for you in a child's distracting behavior. Depending upon the youngster, it may represent one of a variety of communications including "I'm angry", "jealous", "bored" or "anxious".

Forgetting, thoughtlessness or neglecting are all means of letting people know that you really don't like something. What better way than to forget it—like mowing the lawn, doing the dishes, or cleaning a room. Neglecting other people or just being thoughtless about others' rights or needs are some other ways of getting across a point non-verbally. All of these are a means of letting someone know that you are angry, unhappy, disappointed and so on, without stating it in words.

When a child is exhibiting feelings through behavior rather than words, it does not mean that you need to accede to them. It often very helpful to take these non-verbal cues, once you can make sense out of them, and clarify them through verbal communication (convert the communication to words). Sometimes this can clear up a lot of misconceptions. Sometimes it will make clear to the child what his own feelings are, feelings he may not even be aware of until you point them out. And converting non-verbal communication to verbal greatly increases the probability of person-to-person dialogue, and dialogue can solve a world of problems.

In addition to non-verbal communications, there are what we would call *"pre-verbal"* communications. Pre-verbal refers to cues that have to do with use of words, but are not dependent on the words themselves, *or* their definitions, to get the message across. Examples of these are tone of voice, inflection, emphasis on certain words, hesitations, use of certain words or phrases that "push buttons" (set off certain predictable reactions), and activities or behaviors that do the same. If you stop to think about it, most sentences could be said in at least five or six different ways, each with a slightly different meaning depending on tone of voice and emphasis on the individual words. Try this yourself with a simple sentence such as, "I love you." Emphasizing each word separately allows for somewhat different meanings (*I* love you; I *love* you; I love *you*). Then changing the loudness of one's voice adds another dimension. If inflection is also added (feeling "tone", like angry or demanding or loving or tense), something else is communicated, and with certain hesitations in this simple sentence, other meanings occur. The range of messages continues to expand. It should be clear that communication involves a lot more than simply defining the words that are spoken. That is why juries hear live witnesses, not just transcripts of testimony. Another good example of this is to compare reading a play to watching it performed.

Superficial Vs. Sensitive

Another aspect of communication is *superficial vs. sensitive*. A good way to illustrate this is by looking at what happens when our thirteen or fourteen year old child comes up to us with a math test that he has gotten a good grade on. What is our response? Do we glance at it, say something "nice" and then go back to the paper, or do we look at it as an invitation to lay the paper down for a moment and talk about math and anything else related to school or that child's life right now? Oftentimes a child's showing of things are "openings" for communication, and if we don't recognize them as such we pass up opportunities to be in touch with them in a meaningful way as they mature. Kids know when we make ourselves available through an interest in them, and when we do that, they tend to grab hold of the situation and open up to us. They also know when our attention to them is perfunctory or superficial, and they respond accordingly. Think of the times in your life when you were just tolerated or "brushed off", and then remember how it made you feel!

Related to the sensitivity issue, whether communication is *ritualistic vs. spontaneous* reflects the same kind of involvement or lack of involvement. A ritual is a pattern of behavior that has become habitual and a standard routine for a person. A lot of rituals are important. Laying out clothes for the next morning, packing lunches, showering and shaving and brushing teeth in the morning, setting the timer on the coffee pot, and so on, can all be important and convenient rituals. However, when communication becomes ritualized, it can lose something. It can become perfunctory and superficial.

Be aware that when routines which have become well-established (ritualistic) suddenly change, something important may be going on—the change could be a clue to check in with that person. Consider, for example, the youth who has a routine of coming home from school, entering the kitchen, getting a snack, and sitting down at the kitchen table with mom to exchange pleasantries and the day's events. This has established a pattern over time for kid and mom. Suddenly the child stops this pattern. He begins to come home, go to his room and close the door, and spend time there till supper, playing music or just lying on his bed. Clearly this is some indication that this youngster's life has been disrupted in some way. Whether he intends to or not, he has let us know that something has changed. Whether it is good or bad is not always clear. He may be in love, for example, or he may be very sad or upset about something. Such an event may actually impact the whole family system. Mom may worry about it and talk to dad. It may affect how the parents begin to relate to other kids in the family. It is best to communicate directly with the youngster to find out why the change has occurred, so assumptions are not made and people are not jumping to conclusions. Then the parents can make an informed decision as to whether there is something to worry about or not.

Ritualistic behavior has the potential for inhibiting verbal communication in some situations. If a youngster comes home every day after school to have a snack, and that is the time of day that mom has routinely set for watching her soaps without interruption, the child soon learns that he has no effective way of breaking into that pattern and soon stops trying. In time the opportunity for effective verbal communication may be lost. On the other hand, should mom begin to recognize the need for a change in this pattern, tape her soaps to watch at a different time, and make it a point to sit down and be available to her child during, for example, a snack ritual, the child will begin to pick up the change in pattern as a communication that mom is "available" and perhaps will begin to be more open to verbal interchange.

One good rule of thumb in respect to changing others is that if you want to change a certain type of behavior in someone else, change either how you react to that particular behavior, or change whatever you can discover is triggering that behavior in the other person. Take, for example, a thirteen year old we know was acting up in school, being disruptive and carrying on so badly that finally the school suspended him. Previous harangues by parents had not helped. Spankings had not helped. Talking had not helped. What turned out to be effective in changing that behavior was to enroll the youngster in the Funny Bunny Child Care Center for the three-day suspension period. It was a direct commentary on the level of his behavior in school, and as a result, his behavior changed remarkably.

Quantity

Let's look at the notion of quantity in communication, or how much talk is too much talk. Young people frequently comment on the amount of fussing and yakking that they get from their parents, sometimes to the extent that parents feel themselves stereotyped as "lecturers". A good part of this has to do with developmental issues already discussed in the previous chapter. To recap briefly, kids in their teen years have only partially developed the skills to use language, to think abstractly, or to maintain a social ability beyond a rather rude and clumsy style. Their vocabulary banks are limited and they often are not very good conversationalists. Much of their word power consists of a small collection of catch phrases for all occasions, which vary from year to year and generation to generation. Examples of these words and phrases are legion: "Let's boogie", "Cool, man", "I can dig it", "Don't go there", "Radical", "Right on", "Totally awesome", "Been there, done that", "Far out", "Grotey to the max", "Gnarly", "It's bad", and many, many more. Some of these words and phrases take on meanings very different from the original connotations. Sometimes this is because the original meaning wasn't known or was misunderstood, but the word sounded good—and frequent usage changed the meaning for that particular youth subculture. With these notions in mind, let's get back to the lecturing problem. First, we sometimes pour too much on kids at one time. No one likes to be inundated with more than he can handle. In addition, kids are dealing with their own worlds in addition to ours—they often have things other than their relationship with their parents on their minds. When you think of it, teenagers are interacting with several systems of people. They have to deal with parents, home and siblings, with school, and sometimes they have a part-time job which provides yet another group of people. They have a whole system of peers that they interact with, and within that system they have to deal with courtship rituals or at least with flirting and learning how to develop intimate relationships. Frequently they will also be involved in athletics or music or other areas of interest or recreation that helps them to have fun, build self-confidence, and form a sense of identity. With all this in mind, it's a wonder sometimes that we ever do connect successfully with our kids.

When we talk to our kids, we are frequently met with silence. After all, they've been used to listening carefully to adults since an early age, and from about age ten on they've picked up a great deal of their social learning from listening in on adult conversations. Because we're talking to them, even though they are silent, the odds are they're listening. But we fear they are not listening, that they may be tuning us out (they are still not always good at giving us cues), so we keep on talking—and now we're repeating ourselves. We may not be getting any cues that they are listening to us or maybe they are not happy with what we are saying, so they have sullen expressions on their faces as they sit there and listen. And if we continue to get no clear cues, at least verbal ones, we repeat again, and again, and the "lecture" is on. Eventually the kid may say, in effect, "All right, already, I've heard you a dozen times. Do you have to go on and on about it?" And even then we may still not be really certain he really heard it. Sometimes it ends there and sometimes it doesn't. In this situation it is very helpful to find some means of checking out whether the youngster is hearing the message (and do this preferably early in the conversation). Perhaps a simple, "I'm not sure whether you are understanding me—why don't you tell me in your own words what I'm saying, so that I don't end up lecturing." will end the process.

Self Or Other-Directed

Another aspect of communication has to do with whether it is self or other-directed. Many conversations are merely people waiting their turn to say things that they want to say. They aren't necessarily paying close attention to the other person's ideas. Instead, they are busy thinking in their own minds about how they are going to build on the points that they have made in their own previous statement. Such conversation reminds us of conversations on a CB radio, with one person waiting for the other to say "over", so he can hurry up and take his turn to talk. Obviously, this doesn't make for very good communication when one is only interested in sending information and not really interested in receiving any. Communication has the root "co" which implies doing something together—a sharing, a give and take.

The person who routinely seems to have the most success at verbal interaction is the individual who is a "good listener". We've all heard about this type of person, but what makes him or her so appealing? Well, it seems to us that the most outstanding characteristic of a good listener is that this person's attention is "other-directed", that is, he is clearly very much interested in what someone else has to say. How does this impression get across to us? It can happen in a number of ways. First of all, the person is obviously paying close attention and is letting us know that, if they repeat back to us periodically during the conversation, restatements of what we said or some parts of our commentary —that shows us that he is following us. Also he is not acting as though he is in competition with us for speaking time or to get a point across. Persuasion, if it does happen to be part of this person's goal, is usually done in a gentle way and most often through pertinent questions, and the person is generally not highly emotionally charged about the particular topics which he is bringing up in his part of the conversation. If you parents want to be good listeners for your teenagers, look attentive and paraphrase back to them the most important things they tell you. Comments like "so you felt that Lisa was not being fair to you" or "you really felt proud when the coach picked you to pinch hit" will convince any youngster that you are listening and interested!

Affirming Vs. Non-Affirming

The last specific notions in communication we will introduce here relate to being affirming vs. non-affirming in our conversations with our kids. As we are aware from the previous chapter, the teen years are particularly important years in regard to the establishment of identity and a sense of self. It is very important to relate to our youngsters in such a way as to help them build self-confidence, and whenever possible, parents should take an accepting or affirming stance. We need to recall that they are on a ladder of growth, not only physically, but psychologically, emotionally, and socially. Despite body size and physical maturity, they often are very incompletely formed in their skills of thinking and in their abilities relating to talking and interacting with people. Thus, it is important to be positive with them—encouraging their growth by allowing experimentation and tolerating some dumb mistakes, stupid-sounding comments, and downright rudeness (though not always without some firm but gentle directions). Most of us can recall teachers and coaches we had during our grade school or high school years. The ones for whom we were willing to work hardest for were the ones who didn't constantly chew us out for doing things wrong. These were the adults who devoted much time to praising us for the things we did well and worked hard with us to help us correct the things we messed up. Remember, our main job as parents is to be effective as teachers to our kids.

Specific Skills

We now can move on to talking about some specific skills that parents can use when communicating with their youngsters. Their proper use can greatly improve parent-child interactions, and more generally, improve the parent-child relationship.

Modeling

An extremely effective and very commonly used method of teaching is modeling, or "showing by doing". As parents, we do it all the time, though we are often not aware of it. When a new parent starts to deal with his new child, often the first thought that comes to mind is, "What would my mother (or father) have done in this situation?" This is a good example of the modeling (teaching) done by our parents with us as children. We likewise teach our children most of what we teach them by how we ourselves behave, and not so much by what we tell them to do. This is particularly true for moral values and many habit patterns. The father who goes around hitting his kids can expect that the child will be physical in dealing with his peers and probably also with others in the family. The parent who smokes can probably count on the fact that the child will try it (as most kids will) but it also conveys a message that it is okay to do. The parent who drinks excessively gives the message that alcohol is all right and that being impaired by chemicals is also o.k. (and if one drug is "approved", why not others). The parent who says "Don't start this bad habit, look what it does to me", might just as well save his breath for all the good the words will do. Modeling is one of the most powerful teaching tools, although the results are often not seen very immediately. The results are those that may be seen years down the road when you are able to look back and say, "I guess I did that one right! (or wrong!)." One of the strongest modeling messages that can be given by parents is how to not be "perfect". The perfect parent is a myth, but some people hold on to it. A "perfect parent" is one who refuses to recognize his or her mistakes or who refuses to acknowledge responsibility for them, and tends to blame others or external circumstances instead. The "perfect parent" does not allow a child the opportunity to learn by watching, to discover how one can recover from errors, or how one retraces one's steps and does something over again and better, or how one goes back and apologizes for a misjudgment or a false accusation. The child grows up learning the wrong way to handle these things because he has watched it over the years done incorrectly. Sadly, "perfect parents" are often so well defended against seeing their own errors that they are the only ones who don't see them.

Reframing

Reframing is the process of removing something from its familiar context, altering the surroundings to make an idea or notion stand out in a different way. If we take a look at a painting, for example, we generally don't pay much attention to the frame that surrounds it or to the wall that it hangs on. If we change that frame, however, or its placement on the wall or its location in the home, there is sometimes a striking difference in how we see that same picture. It may hit us completely differently or just be more pleasant or unpleasant. Reframing ideas can have much the same result. Borrowing from an old joke, consider for example the two boys who are both brought to the same closed door and told there will be a surprise. When the door is opened and the room is found to be full of horse manure, the first boy feels offended and stomps off angrily. From his perspective, he has been dealt a dirty trick. The other boy, however, yells "Oh boy!" and wades cheerfully into the room. "With all this horse manure, there must be a pony in here somewhere!" The same two boys might look at a partially-filled glass of water, and one would claim it was half-empty while the other might call it half-full. It all depends on one's perspective, one's "frame" of reference.

Reframing is essentially a communication tool to help others change their perspective. It is a means of putting someone's feelings into a different background so that he can experience them differently. A frequent problem that teenagers have with perception is that things seem to occur in extremes, black and white, all or none, and so on, and often only one part of something is focused on at a time. In reframing, the idea is to show another view by introducing previously unseen elements, to make the new view visible along with the old. For example, consider a young man that has been dating a girl for several weeks. He seems to be "falling in love" and one night they get involved in some heavy petting. Over the next several days he seems to be in conflict, appearing emotionally troubled. He spends less time with the girl, he's more irritable around the house, and he seems preoccupied. He's never been very wordy with his parents, so one day his father asks, "John, is something going on between you and Cindy?" John replies, "Ah, I just don't know if I really like her that much anymore." As part of several comments about relationships with the opposite sex Dad says, "Sometimes when guys get to liking a girl a lot, it makes the hormones flow and you can get a little scared. Every girl, like a guy, has a physical side, too, and it's bound to come out when people get close. It's up to both the boy and the girl to keep the physical part where it's under control and feels comfortable. I don't know if that's what 's going on between you and Cindy, but I wouldn't be surprised." John says, "Thanks, Dad." Dad then has the good sense not to pursue a long conversation or give a bunch of explanations with John. He made a statement that shows some understanding of what is upsetting his son, he does not pry for details, but he shows that he is open to discussing it further if John should want to do so. Dad also reframed the "good girl/ bad girl" split by comparing them to guys (whom John knows better) and by pointing to the boy's need for participation in setting limits on the physical expression of their love. He doesn't expect an answer from John; as part of teaching his son about life and relationships he just wants this message to reach him. Reframing is a very useful technique for many of the situations that disturb teenagers. Parents can bring a more experienced, broader, more accepting perspective to a lot of different problems. "Have you considered looking at it this way?", "Can I give you a little different perspective on that?" and "Another way of thinking about this situation" are all examples of reframing "lead-ins". Start with a well-conceived, non-threatening lead-in (in your own words) and the rest will flow intuitively.

Reassurance

Reassurance is a skill that comes pretty naturally to some people, but like any habit, it has to be learned. It can be a very useful aid to communication with youth because it carries with it a sense of trust and hope that allows for more openness. It is important to be able to reassure our kids about the things that they are doing well. It gives them regular feedback on their behavior, helping them to benefit from their experiences, and it contributes to positive self-esteem. It is very important not to get caught up in the kind of parent-child relationship where all or most of the feedback given to children is negative, just "bad boy" or "bad girl" stuff. There needs to be lots of "good boy" and "good girl" complete with clear elaboration of what was good. And when they stray from "goodness", help them out, and reassure them that they are "good persons" and that they will benefit from their experiences. If they know that we give feedback when due, and that we will give reassurance when appropriate, they often will ask for it, opening the door to lots of conversation and communication.

Humor

Humor is vital if we want to effectively teach our kids, and an important form of humor is to be able to laugh at ourselves—not all the time, but once in a while. A sure way to alienate young people is to take ourselves too seriously, to try to convince them that we think we are "perfect". This goes back to modeling. If we can't teach our kids that occasionally what we do is ridiculous or stupid or funny, how can we expect them to accept the same in themselves? And we all know that some of the things they do are funny. If we can learn to laugh at ourselves, we'll be able to find a lot of humorous things to interact with our kids about, and this makes us more accessible to them. Unfortunately, we have seen in our office whole families unable to laugh about themselves. All of these individuals, including the teenagers, are caught up in trying to be above human fallibilities, in trying to appear "perfect". Egos are fragile, and any implication of imperfection can be emotionally devastating. We feel like saying things like "loosen up", "relax", "you're an o.k. person, can't you see that", and "we can accept your shortcomings, so you should too". However, for these individuals, change comes only with a lot of work and not through simple dictates from anyone.

I-messages

To effectively communicate, we need to get our ideas across. However, this can be difficult if our words sound accusatory or demeaning or we say things in other ways that make it difficult for the hearer to listen past the first sentence without getting angry or defensive. One very important notion to keep in mind is that if we talk about ourselves, our own feelings and our own preferences, we are less likely to irritate or alienate others than if we focus our comments on them. The term "I-messages" refers to statements about one's self (and avoidance of accusatory or other "you" statements). Some examples of I-messages in typical parent-teenager situations are: "I have concerns about your being out so late."; "I find it hard to face a lot of questions when I first walk in the door." and "I get discouraged when I have to repeat the rules over and over." Some examples of common you-messages are: "You're dragging in at all hours again"; "You left me a big mess in the kitchen"; "you sure loused that up"; "Don't pester me the minute I walk in the door"; and "You keep doing the same thing over and over." The I-messages tend to get our ideas across more effectively, creating less emotional resistance in our kids than "you this and that". At the same time, I-messages also communicate to the youngster that he is responsible for changing his own behavior—it implies a trust that he will assume that responsibility, and that we are giving him the opportunity to do so.

Negotiation

Whenever an animal gets cornered, no matter how timid it normally may be, its tendency is to fight. Many of the great diplomats of the world have recognized that great victories can be won without bloodshed as long as some means of honor is left to the loser. With these two notions in mind, one can see that negotiation with your child is important, knowing that it generally is not useful to back him into a corner that he cannot get out of, or at least learn something from. Negotiating does not mean giving up a position of power or capitulating, and it certainly does not mean being "perfect" or condescending. Negotiating means listening to another position, accepting the fact that there may be at least some merit to that position, and making some decision about whether to make concessions or compromises. In order to be an effective communicator and teacher, the pupil has to be accessible, and sometimes negotiation is very helpful in laying the groundwork for that accessibility. All good parents are good negotiators. You want your daughter in at 10 o'clock, she wants to come in at 2 a.m. because some of her friends stay out all night, how about midnight? This negotiation should be done in the context of a give and take conversation, both sides expressing their fears, concerns, desires, and so on, giving both sides the sense that the other understands their position and care enough to try to make the situation o.k. for everybody.

Paraphrasing

Paraphrasing or "active listening" is a communication tool that sounds easy but takes a certain amount of practice to use consistently and effectively. It amounts to making short, concise restatements of what the other person is saying. It is a means of very clearly letting the other person know that you are actively listening to him/her and identifies the feelings which accompany the experiences which the teller is relating. Imagine yourself at a movie. You see a series of pictures or images which tell a story, and the story has a beginning, middle and ending. There are characters, a plot, and a setting. Paraphrasing can be likened to a movie, or better yet, to a slide show in the hearer's head. The chief character is the teller, and the listener forms the images (slides) and comments on them to let the teller know he is being attentive. These comments should be brief, should contain facts and feelings, and should concentrate on the teller's experiences. Paraphrasing should let the teller know, "This is what I have understood from what you're saying." It should say, "I heard you; I'm with you; I understand; please go on." It is important to realize that questions and opinions tend to interfere with the paraphrasing process and may actually have the opposite effect, appearing interruptive. Given below is an example of paraphrasing.

> Teller: "Man oh man, am I bushed. The PE teacher had us run ten laps, then we played basketball for thirty minutes, and then we lifted weights."

> Listener: "Sounds like quite a workout."

> Teller: "Then I went to English class and had to give an extemporaneous speech with only five minutes preparation."

Listener: "That's not a lot of time to prepare."

Teller: "But I got an 'A' for the work, and he's a tough teacher."

Listener: "That must leave you with a sense of accomplishment."

Teller: "Well, the rest of the day didn't go as smoothly. I had a fight Mary and thought about it all day, but then we made up after our last class."

Listener: "Well it certainly sounds like an exciting day. I'm glad things worked out well in the end."

Now, here is an example of poor listening skills, evidenced in part by no paraphrasing:

Teller: "Man oh man, am I bushed. The PE teacher had us run ten laps, then we played basketball for thirty minutes, and then we lifted weights."

Listener: "He sounds like my old gym teacher. Did he make you do bear crawls across the gym? Ours used to do that, then make us run laps the whole period. I used to get so tired, I hated that guy!"

Teller: "Well he's not that bad. Oh, I got an 'A' in English class for a speech I did."

Listener: " Is that the same teacher Monica had two years ago? She was pretty interested in making people do speeches as I remember."

Teller: "Nah, different teacher. What's for supper?"

Metaphor

A metaphor is the application of a word or phrase to an object or concept which it does not literally denote. It's used to suggest comparison or provide a description (like for example, "a mighty fortress is our God."). Metaphors are commonly used for communicative purposes. They employ symbols and imagery that make ideas stand out in a different way and thus can make reframing more distinct. Images that are familiar are often more useful to make a point, and imagery that appeals to different senses often strikes home in a special way. Combined with an appropriate dose of reasonable humor, imagery and metaphors can be helpful, but be very careful to avoid sarcasm and cynicism. Below are some examples of the communicating power of the metaphor.

> "Jason has a brain like a sponge. He just looks at a science book and soaks up the information."

> "Bill, you're as tense as a banjo string."

> "Cathy, when you whine that way, you're like a violin out of tune."

> "Joe, you need to be more clear. What you're saying sounds like plaids, stripes and polka dots all on the same shirt."

Psychological Theories About Communication

The final group of ideas that we would like to present in this chapter come from some well-known psychological theories. Although hundreds of theorists have addressed issues of communication, we have chosen some bits and pieces from a few selected works that hopefully will add to the base of knowledge and skills we have already discussed. This is not intended to be a complete survey or a detailed restatement of these theories. The information below has been selected for its simplicity and its relevance specifically to the parenting of teenagers.

There have been many volumes written by *Sigmund Freud* and since his death, about Sigmund Freud. He wrote extensively regarding his perceptions of the structure of personality and the workings of the human mind. He differentiated three parts which he called the id, the ego and the superego, and he described in detail how they were formed and how they operated. Very significant in his work, at least in regard to communication, would seem to be his grasp of the concept of the "unconscious". Freud became aware that some things are too painful to the human mind to stay in conscious awareness for very long. Yet these things seemed to continue to affect the behavior of the person even though he couldn't remember them. Freud said that these incidents remained in the memory, but at an "unconscious level." He felt he was able in various ways, including hypnosis, to draw this material out of the unconscious. He speculated that these unconscious thoughts were kept there by an active defense process called "repression" and that these thoughts were not readily available to the individual. Freud elaborated on his notions of the unconscious in his treatment of wit and parapraxes (slips of the tongue). He pointed out that thoughts we have in our unconscious can sometimes "slip out" in the form of jokes, slips of the tongue, dreams and other seemingly harmless ways. We can find ourselves, for example, humming a tune which may have a great deal to do with some inner thoughts, without being aware of the connection between the thoughts and the words of the song until later. The notions of the unconscious and its means of expression are very useful as part of an overall understanding of communication. It tells us that there is more to what people are thinking and saying than just "what's on the surface". It also suggests that where there are underlying and "hidden" meanings in someone's communication, so that a person may not even be aware of them. For example, a teenager whose father left the family at a very early age, when saying she "hates" her male homeroom teacher may really be telling us how angry she is at dad for abandoning them. Some unconscious-directed communications are not very deep and devious, and can be recognized by the attentive and concerned parent. What is your teenager trying to tell you and why? The reasons may be a little below the surface.

Another communication model is that which comes from *Learning Theory*. Some of what has already been presented earlier in this book comes from this body of thought. It is often called a "behavioral model" and refers to thinking about behaviors including communication in terms of reactions to things ("responses" to "stimuli") in our environment. Technically, learning is defined as "the process which changes the probability that a given response will follow a given stimulus". If there is positive reinforcement (a reward) for a particular behavior, the chances are good that the behavior will be repeated. Consider the example of the girl whose mother cannot spend much time with her except when teaching her sewing. The girl learns to look forward to the times with mother (they are rewarding) and probably learns to sew quite well. Just as surely, a person who puts his hand on a hot stove learns rapidly that it is not a good idea. If there is a negative result (a punishment) every time an activity occurs, the chances are good that the behavior will not be repeated. Interestingly enough, it has been discovered that if a negative impact on a particular behavior is given most of the time, but occasionally a notable positive impact occurs, the probability of the behavior repeating can be very high. For example, the child who filches cookies may be caught and punished numerous times, but if he occasionally gets away with a few of the sweet morsels, the chance he'll go for more is high. A person playing slot machines may lose most of the time, but when he hits a jackpot once every 10-15 times, it is enough to keep him spinning the wheels.

A man named Burris F. Skinner experimented with animals and found that if he rewarded certain behaviors as they naturally occurred, he could train the animals to do those behaviors by adding cues. For example, he trained pigeons to dance in circles in a particular direction by rewarding (with food pellets) their natural movements in that direction. He would light up a light bulb in their cages prior to dropping food and would wait for the pigeons to turn further in a particular direction before he would release the food. Once they began to turn for the food, he would require them to turn further and further until they had turned one or more circles, before he would reward them. After awhile, he merely had to turn on the cue light and they would start spinning. He was able to apply these "teaching" techniques to other animals.

It is said that Skinner's students once played a trick on him, pretending to be bored as he lectured. He apparently had a tendency to walk back and forth on the stage from which he lectured, and whenever he walked to the right side of the stage, the boredom of the students with their yawning and inattention was rampant. However as he walked over to the left side of the stage, their attention brightened up, they became more alert, and were obviously interested. As he walked back to the right, the boredom increased again. By the end of the hour, he allegedly was spending all his time standing on the left addressing his students who were giving him all their attention. As the rumor goes, Skinner never caught on, at least that day.

There are many implications here for communication. As we work with our kids to teach them the things about life and relationships we think are important, we must be able to communicate our feelings. We give our rewards and punishments to help them learn. Much of what we do in raising our kids is to reward their behaviors that we like, including their attempts to communicate, in order that we see more of those behaviors. Obviously, desired behaviors can be reinforced by words, but also by a variety of non-verbal communications such as attention or listening posture. Often a smile at the right moment, a wink, or a pleasant look will do the trick as well or better than words.

There is a very important principle of modifying behavior that comes from learning theory: Positive reinforcement (reward) of a desired behavior is much more effective and long-lasting than negative reinforcement (punishment) of an undesired behavior. The results are much better if a parent focuses on and rewards the behaviors they want to see, than if they punish what they don't want. A lot of us who were involved in sports as teenagers can remember the best coaches we had. Usually they were the ones who were encouraging us, not putting us down. Those that encouraged us, we were ready to work for; the punishers were the ones we tried to outwit. The same processes occur between us and our kids. In situations that are very important or have potentially serious outcomes, one may consider the approach called "counter-conditioning". With two opposing behaviors, one undesirable and one desirable, both punish the undesirable and reward the desirable. *For example, if you need to help your child to establish better homework habits, reward his sitting down and opening the books with praise, allowance, later curfew, or similar advantages. Negatively approach his coming home and watching television or talking at length on the phone to friends (instead of hitting the books) with negative statements, earlier curfew, or restriction of privileges.* However, as much as possible, you should focus on the reward part of this model for teaching, keeping punishment brief and relevant, but elaborating any chance you get to mete out rewards.

There has grown up over the past couple of decades a large body of theory on the issue of *assertiveness*. It relates contrasting ways of approaching interpersonal relationships, defining one ("assertive") as the best for everyone involved. People who teach "assertiveness training" say that to be assertive rather than manipulative, submissive, aggressive or hostile enhances personal relationships and ultimately enriches one's life. To be assertive is to invite negotiation; it is to function in an equal, side by side, position with another individual. Assertiveness requires that you stand up for your personal rights in a direct, honest, and appropriate manner, in ways which do not violate other people's rights.

There are three basic assumptions to accept if you intend to practice assertive behavior: 1) People are not out to get you; 2) People are doing the best they know how to do; and 3) People are basically cooperative and helpful. Obviously, there are some situations where these premises do not fit, but for the most part in families, at work, and with peers, they do.

In order to be assertive, you have to establish "body control"—direct eye contact, body posture appropriate to the situation, controlled breathing, appropriate gestures, facial expression consistent with your message, and an appropriate voice tone, inflection, and volume. A consideration of timing is also important. Is it an appropriate time to be attempting this communication? Finally, attention to the content of the message is also necessary.

One approach to defining assertive **behavior** is to contrast it with other less desirable options. It is important to know the differences between aggressive, assertive, acquiescent, and non-assertive behaviors. *"Aggressiveness"* is defined as a dominating, non-negotiable posture. It typically "shuts down" the other person; it is often a "getting back" stance. It usually shuts off any possibility of give and take communication. Aggressive behavior may include: Answering before the other person is finished speaking; speaking loudly and/or abusively; glaring at the other person; speaking "past the issue", which includes accusing, blaming and demeaning the other person; valuing yourself above the other person; and hurting others to avoid hurting yourself. The parent-child relationship where one or both of the individuals approach the other aggressively is usually characterized by one-way communication, lack of openness, hard feelings, and so on.

Assertiveness is a "working through it" stance. It is a striving to keep communication channels open. It is a self-expression without hurting others. It maximizes the communication process between two individuals. Assertiveness is to make one's feelings and purpose clear while maintaining a posture of negotiation. Assertive behavior includes: Answering spontaneously while staying with the issues; speaking with conversational tone and volume; speaking to the issues; openly expressing personal feelings and opinions (including anger, love, sorrow, and disagreement) in a manner which is not hurtful to others or meant to induce guilt; valuing yourself as equal to others; and maintaining a negotiating stance. When properly applied by both parties in a parent-teenager relationship, assertiveness very often leads to clear and open communication, understanding, problem-solving and the kind of adult-child connection that pleases everyone.

"Acquiescence" implies that you're truly willing to go along. It is a conflict-avoidance posture. It may become a problem when mutual responsibility is needed or when one is in charge of another person.

"Non-assertiveness" is an extreme "going along with it" stance, regardless of one's own feelings. Non-assertive behavior includes: Hesitating; speaking very softly; looking away; avoiding the issues; agreeing, regardless of your own feelings, and not expressing your own opinions; valuing yourself "below" others; and hurting yourself to avoid any chance of hurting others. Carried to its extreme, non-assertiveness is constant and complete submissiveness, with none of the give and take which characterized good communication.

The last theoretical notions that will be discussed in this chapter come from the work of an intriguing group of people who worked in Palo Alto in the 1950's and continue to the present. The original four, Bateson, Jackson, Haley and Weakland published an important report called, "Toward a Theory of

Schizophrenia" . In that paper they described various communication patterns, noting that some are instrumental in producing serious emotional disturbances. Some of the most interesting notions that have been elaborated by this group and others who have followed, have to do with *"metacommunication"*, referring to communication at different levels of abstraction. When we speak of different levels of abstraction, we refer to the fact that things can be expressed or received literally (what the words mean) or more abstractly (as in a play on words). A message can be given, for example, which states the words, "I love you", but the tone of voice, inflection, facial expression or body posture may give the opposite message. When a teacher smiles and warmly says "good job" after you answer a question in front of the class, the meaning is literal and pleasant. When someone says "good job" with a distinctly sarcastic tone of voice, it has a meaning quite contrary to the literal one above. It expresses "way to mess up", actually meaning "bad job".

The notion of the *paradox* has been studied at length by the Palo Alto group. Paradox has a dictionary definition as a statement or proposition seemingly self-contradictory or absurd, but in reality expressing a possible truth. Paradoxical statements tend to make people stand back and look again. Examples of paradoxical statements would include: "Why don't you keep dating so you can find out what you don't like about her." and "I don't want you to quit your job until you prove you can't handle it." In both statements there is more being communicated than is apparent on the surface. Paradoxes cause us to do a "double take". They have an effect much like metaphors but are more potent because of the initial confusion effect or "surprise". You have to hear them twice! A famous hypnotherapist who was very influential on the thinking of the Palo Alto Group described a confusion and surprise technique in inducing hypnosis, illustrating the power of such approaches in gaining people's attention. Since attention is basic to establishing communication, it is not surprising that the use of paradox can be very effective.

Throughout this chapter we have attempted not only to define communication through discussion of concepts, skills, and theories, but to show its tremendous importance in the human experience. It is fundamental to any relationship and your exploration of your relationships with your children should always be attentive to communication. Through effective communication you both teach them what you want them to know as well as getting along harmoniously while doing so.

Pearls For Parents:

1) We tend to be verbal animals, and the language that we use to think about ourselves is important in establishing our self-concept. If we were to look around the room at any object, we immediately have a name for that object—desk, chair, TV, book, lamp, window, and so on. Everything that we look at has a verbal symbol to go with it. We think in words, and the words we use influence us a great deal in *how* we think. Thus it is very important to think about the selection of words that we use in dealing with our kids, and it is also extremely important to not get into name calling or labeling in a negative fashion with our kids. Whether they let on or not, our verbal messages to our kids affect them greatly. If a kid routinely thinks of himself as dumb, bad, or clumsy, he will tend to act in such a way as to live up to those expectations.

2) Many of the decisions that are made as children, with children's reasoning, tend to stay with us for many years, unless those decisions are re-examined and re-decided at a time when we can come to a more mature conclusion. A child, for example, who is told by a teacher that his art work is not what it should be may make the decision that he is just not a good artist, and stop trying. Whenever possible, parents need to keep a child's options to learn free and open, in order that he or she may continue to grow in many and varied ways as they mature.

3) Unless we are writing for others to read or carrying on a conversation, we tend to think in phrases and images. Imagine taking a long afternoon's driving trip and getting to the end of the trip. If someone asked, "What did you learn during your drive?" the reply might be, "lots of cows, mountains were beautiful, got sleepy", or something similar. However, if you had made

the trip with a companion, the answer to that question might be quite different, because, in order to carry on a conversation with a companion and to make sense of it, one has to speak in complete sentences. One sentence follows another and thoughts are built on one another. In order to effectively communicate, thoughts and ideas have to build on each other. This is why it is important to "talk through" things with our kids. An ideal parent-child interaction involves an extended give and take expression of ideas within the context of an emotionally positive and mutually respectful relationship.

4) Remember that all people do not think in the same way that we do. Do not assume that because we know that the most reasonable way for us to get something done is in some particular way, that it is so for everyone else on the planet. There is more than one way to skin a cat, so they say, and people make decisions from different perspectives and from different experiences. That is certainly often the case with our kids. *Take, for example, the farmer's son watching his dad try to push a stubborn calf through a barnyard gate. The farmer, exasperated and angry that his son is laughing at his non-productive efforts, tells the kid to get the calf through the gate himself if he is so smart. The kid jumps off the fence, grabs the calf by the tail and pulls. As the stubborn calf pulls back, the boy lets go of the tail, and the calf ambles through on his own momentum.*

A good lesson for parents is not to take themselves too seriously; if they do, their kids often won't.

Sometimes people make dumb choices, and that also can be the case with kids. Sometimes because of personal history, or lack thereof, people just have a different point of view.

5) In spite of our verbal abilities, words are sometimes insufficient. Remember, showing is better than telling—a "picture" can be worth a thousand words!

6) Don't waste a lot of time asking kids why they did something (they will often say, "I don't know" anyway). Clearly communicate to them what you want them to do and what you want

them not to do. And don't forget to give them rewards, verbal or otherwise, when they choose to do what you want them to do.

7) Remember that kids have to make choices too, especially as they get into their teen years and start exploring the world more. Parents need not take responsibility for all that their kids do or don't do, but it is important to let them know where you stand in order to impart your sense of values and tradition. Remember that modeling is a great teaching tool, and that lecturing often is not very effective.

8) It is important to remember that the role of parents is not just to be friends with our teenagers. That is fine if it works out that way, but it is also important to know when to back off the role of being a pal and resume the role again of being a manager. It can happen in a split second, and it can be very reassuring to the kids. They are not always going to be operating at the same level of psychological development as we are, and certainly not with the same level of life experience. If we tend to debate with our kids when they are operating at a different level of understanding, we are functioning at the lowest common denominator, at their level. Remember it is not what a child of 14 or 15 thinks of us this moment that we should be worried about, but what they will think of us when they are 24 or 25. If a particular situation requires that you, as the adult, take charge, then do it. In the long run, it is best for your kids.

9) Sometimes it is important not to give kids too many choices, or they can drive you nuts making a decision. For example, you might not want to say, "What do you want for breakfast?" or they may give you the menu at the Hilton. Instead, make it easy, like "Do you want Rice Krispies or Corn Flakes?" This is a simple communication, one which clearly requires only a simple response (one of two options).

10) Remember that timing is very important. If you want to enhance the possibility that something will work out, it is important to have a sense of when to talk about it. This is not to

say that we should "walk around on eggshells", but sometimes difficult topics become easier if we wait for the right moment to broach them. For example, if your youngster just an hour ago learned he didn't make the starting squad on his baseball team, help him deal with that disappointment now, and leave your agenda of his coming home late last Saturday night for another day.

11) Pick your fights. It is a good rule of thumb in marriages as well as in parenting. Choose the things that are worth fighting about.

12) The best way to change behaviors in others is generally to change the manner in which we react to those behaviors.

13) We all learn from our mistakes. Model for your kids how you deal with your own mistakes. For example, "That grounding I gave you yesterday was too long. I was angry, but I thought about it and decided to cut the grounding from 2 weeks to one weekend." Allow your kids to make mistakes, in order to learn from them, but try to choose situations where the mistakes are least dangerous, when you can.

14) Try, when you can, to structure success for your kids. Maneuver the situation when you can, to allow for a positive outcome, and praise the result.

Resources:

Books
How Real Is Real? by Paul Watzlawick, Ph.D.
Vintage Books (division of Random House), New York, 1976

The Language of Change by Paul Watzlawick, Ph.D.
Basic Books, Inc. 1978

Situation Hopeless But Not Serious by Paul Watzlawick, Ph.D. W.W.Norton & Co., New York, 1983

Ultra-solutions by Paul Watzlawick, Ph.D.
W.W.Norton & Co., New York, 1988

Born To Win by Muriel James and Dorothy Jongeward
Addison-Wesley Publishing Company Reading, Massachusetts, 1971

Making Sense of Adolescence—How to Parent From
The Heart by John Crudele, C.S.P. and Richard Erickson Ph.D. Triumph Books, Liquore, Missouri 1995

Parenting Teens With Love and Logic by Foster Cline, M.D.
and Jim Fay Pinon Press, Colorado Springs, Colorado, 1992

Men Are From Mars;_Women Are From Venus by John
Gray, Ph.D. Harper Collins Publishers, 1992

Classic Movies:

Twelve Angry Men (Henry Fonda, Lee J. Cobb)

Do The Right Thing (Spike Lee movie)

The Remains of the Day (Anthony Hopkins, Emma Thompson)

Shadowlands (Anthony Hopkins, Debra Winger)

Cinderella Man (Russell Crow)

Chapter 4
FAMILY RELATIONSHIPS

"Never let someone outside the family know what you are thinking."
— **The Godfather**

The vast majority of people we encounter through life come from families. These are most often families including at least one, and usually two or more, biologically related human beings. The influence of this social unit, the family, is without equal in the formation of the human personality. The family pervasively effects how we think, how we feel, and how we act. It generally begins its influence when we are a newborn baby, a "tabula rasa" (a "blank slate"), and teaches us things that profoundly affect us for the rest of our life. This chapter presents some varying perspectives on the family, some different ways to view and understand it.

The Family As Culture
The word "family" carries its own meaning to different people. To some, it refers only to very close relatives; to others, it denotes extended family with aunts and uncles, grandparents, cousins, distant cousins and clans; to yet others, it means the close group of friends, related or not, that one dearly loves and wants to be associated with. However we view it and whomever we include in our own personal sense of family, the notion of family brings with it the concept of culture. One definition of culture offered in the Random House Dictionary is "the sum total of ways of living built up by a group of human beings and

transmitted from one generation to another." This notion of culture can certainly be applied to vast geographic regions and to nations, but it also is an accurate definition for "subcultures" such as African-American, Asian-American, Eastern European, Gay, Transgender, and so on. Looking at smaller logical sub-groupings of people who transmit "ways of living" from one generation to another, the family must certainly be included. It is not within the scope of this book to look at all the various cultures or subcultures in our world and how they differ from one another—we will focus on the American family as a form of culture.

Our American heritage is replete with a sense of family as the basic unit of our society. Thus, our culture treats the family as the fundamental building block. If we extend the notion of culture down to the individual family, we see that our overall American culture is made up of a patchwork quilt of over a million family cultures, each affected by the influence of its particular heritage, its unique history.

What are the various family-related things that combine to make a culture? *Traditions* are an important ingredient. Traditions may be defined as habitual patterns of behavior, regular and repeated ways of doing things. Sometimes, the original reasons for the existence of those patterns may be lost. I remember the story of an individual who, whenever cooking a ham at Easter, always cut off the butt before putting it in the roaster for cooking. When asked why she did that, she said that her mother had always done so, and since her mother had taught her how to cook, she followed the tradition. My inquiry made her curious, so later when the opportunity arose, she asked her mother why she always cut off the butt. Her mother replied that it was because she never had a roasting pot big enough to hold the whole ham. The tradition had started out of a pragmatic need, and then, even when the need was gone, it had continued down through the family. Parents routinely pass on "ways of doing things" to their children, and thus, traditions continue through the generations.

Though many traditions arise out of patterns in our larger cultures, such as traditional dress (which may have arisen out of climactic needs or available goods) or traditional foods (again which may have arisen out of availability, cost and/or ease of preparation in the particular circumstances), others have arisen out of the cultural context of our family's patterns of *religion*. We tend to follow the habits and patterns of our particular denomination, out of our own choice—this is another aspect of culture in which we find ourselves participating. We also tend to have certain sociological and economic beliefs and leanings, depending on the particular family culture in which we are raised. This inclines us to gravitate toward one or another *political philosophy* or belief system. There are lots of options here, from ultra-conservative to ultra-liberal, and everything in between. Still another aspect of culture that is often prominent is the sense of *work ethic* and the development of work skills that impact on the inhabitants of the family as culture. *Discipline* is yet another aspect of culture. Not only is there the notion of how discipline is maintained and administered toward one another, but how each individual in the family maintains control of oneself and manages one's own behavior.

Rituals are a significant and important means of establishing personal identity, family connection, and the sense of culture in a family. They provide a connection to past generations, to present family members, and to future choices and interactions. They help us to move through the passages of life, to endure and survive losses, and to celebrate and affirm life. There are the day-to-day rituals, such as how and when we eat, who reads the bedtime stories, what the standard morning preparations for the day are and what are the behaviors seen when getting ready for bed. There are lots of ways to get these things done. You could look at a hundred families and no two would handle them exactly the same. There are also holiday rituals, seasonal rituals, and other special occasion rituals. They mark milestones in the family's life events, like birthdays, weddings, anniversaries, graduations and funerals. And there are uncounted ways to mark these milestones. Just think about the way your family handles them; then look at other families. Does a birthday require a cake, a party, a card, a present, a surprise, a meal, or some combination of these or other possibilities? We heard of one family who required the singing of "Happy Birthday" at 12:01 am on the day of the birthday! Families develop their own patterns and then pass them down from one generation to the next. Rituals are very important to the family sense of culture. They foster predictability and greatly increase a sense of unity in the family.

When we look at the family and its culture, we become aware that in addition to the effects of our extended culture defined by religion (such as Mormon, Catholic, Islam, Protestant or Jewish) or defined by ethnic background (such as Italian, Irish, Japanese or Russian) we all carry a closer and more recent history of our own families into our daily lives. The experiences of parents and grandparents, also in the context of their own personal microcultures, impact a great deal on the lives of their children. In our families we all develop a sense of tradition, of religious belief, of political awareness, of expectations around discipline and of a work ethic, and this varies remarkably from family to family.

The culture of family is not rigid or set for centuries, however. Through marriage, families mix, and of course there are always the ongoing influences of the larger cultural groups such as neighborhood, city or state, church, political affiliation, and schools. Because of this mixing, family cultures tend to evolve and change over time. There is a "natural" resistance to change for almost any kind of social unit, and that includes the family, so in the absence of extremely dramatic and traumatic influences, change is usually gradual and predictable.

Family As System

One way to visualize a "system" is to think of it as a machine. Each part depends upon all the other parts for the overall optimal functioning of the whole. A bee hive is a system; so is a business corporation; and so is a family. Systems are essentially interdependent units, structured either accidentally or purposefully to work together, generally in a cooperative fashion, to achieve a common goal. When we look at a system, we must look at its characteristics. These include: The power structure (who makes the rules, who is in charge), the kinds of communication, how problems get solved and decisions are made, the values in the system, the various interdependencies that exist, and the roles that are played by various members, and how stable all these definitions are.

Family systems can be based on "traditional" models (where the father is the principle breadwinner and the mother is the principle homemaker), or on one of the models that have become common in the last several decades, a less traditional variation (for example, where there are two equal breadwinners and the homemaking duties are shared, or where there is a single parent, or where there are same sex parents, or where producing income and doing household chores are divided equally among numerous family members with division of chores among family members). We will take a look below at some family system characteristics, variables which can help us to differentiate and better understand our society's families.

Assumption of Roles

Various individuals play different roles at different times, even within a "healthy" family system. A father in a traditional family system, for example, may make the decision about when to buy a new car, but he will not interfere with his wife's decision about how to decorate the living room. This is not to say that each will gather input from the other (like "do you think we need a bigger car to accommodate the kids' friends?" or "what do you think about getting rid of the curtains and getting blinds?"), but in this traditional model dad is expected to take care of the car-buying details and mom will work on the details for house decoration. In less traditional systems, a common one requires that decisions are discussed more, sometimes argued about, but settled in a more "democratic" way, one that is less dependent on strict roles. Yet roles still play a part, though in a more subtle manner. The other non-traditional scenario sometimes encountered finds one person essentially making virtually all decisions, with little or no significant input from other family members. Each family works out its assumption of roles, based upon the personalities and desires of the family members as well as the expectations passed down from previous generations (as discussed earlier in this chapter).

Though some roles tend to be fairly firm, deriving from the individual cultures that each adult was raised in, they also tend to evolve over time. A good example of this evolution can be more easily seen in the children, though it also happens, sometimes more subtly, in adults. The child first takes on the role of "the baby". Then the child becomes "mother's little helper". Next he or she becomes the "big sister or big brother". The child then becomes, in addition, the "big kid going off to school". Some kids become "the jock"; others become "the scholar"; still others "the prankster" or "the smooth talker". One of the concerns about roles is that they can tend to stick to a kid who accepts that role, and generally it is healthier to teach kids to shift roles so that they don't get locked in. Even that kid who gets a lot of positive reinforcement and a sense of positive self-esteem from being a good athlete or a good scholar should learn that he is not solely limited to that arena of activity to get the good things out of life. We remember one child, for example, who was a good athlete, but he had a serious injury that limited his athletic endeavors for the future. Fortunately he had developed other skills, and he commented, "I learned that it is good to have other things besides your body to depend on."

In less healthy families, roles tend to be considerably more entrenched. Some kids become *scapegoats,* being labeled as the "bad kid", the "clumsy kid", or some other negative appellation. In early biblical history, at a certain time of year a goat was symbolically given the sins of the community to carry with him as he was driven out to the desert to die. Unfortunately, in some family systems individuals are sometimes "designated" as people who deserve derision—thus the word scapegoat. Such roles tend to take most of the heat off other family members and focus it on the one designated individual. One enduring problem is that the kid who gets the label of scapegoat often tends to buy into it over time and to accept it. Then he or she tries, consciously or unconsciously to live up to the family's negative expectations, as any good kid will do. Kids tend to make decisions about themselves based on what they have been told by adults.

Unfortunately, they don't always double back and re-examine those decisions as they get older, in the light of more experience, so they go on thinking of themselves in the same way that they were told as children. If it is essentially negative (inherent in the definitions created for scapegoats), it can color their perceptions of themselves and the manner in which they behave toward others for a good part of their lives.

An important chore for mental health professionals working with families in distress is to sort out the various roles being played by all the various family members. Of special interest is the identification of scapegoating. Once identified, it is to the advantage of all family members, and especially important to the scapegoat, that the behavior is understood and minimized.

Communication

A previous chapter was focused on several different aspects of communication, but the importance of healthy communication within a family system cannot be overstated. Negative statements directed at our kids will often do the opposite of what we want, though sometimes it feels necessary to get all over our kids for the things they do wrong or poorly. However, it generally just doesn't do much good. Studies have shown that positive reinforcement for things done well goes a lot further to encourage the desired behavior than does negative reinforcement for the things poorly done. Stated in another way, words of praise go a lot further than a chewing out.

How families communicate is variable. With some families, the words are clear as a bell. The kids know what Dad wants; because he says it like it is, clearly and concisely. In other families, the kids may often have to "read between the lines". Dad walks into the kitchen and says, "There are going to have to be some changes around here." The kids have learned that this means they need to get busy and put the dishes in the dishwasher and sweep the kitchen floor because years ago he designated them as responsible for the post-meal cleanup.

Sometimes parents say one thing and mean something completely different. A group of mental health professionals referred to in the chapter on communication (Bateson and his colleagues) formulated a "theory of mental illness" based on a communication model called the "Double Bind" (if you would like details on this work, see _Toward a Theory of Schizophrenia_). This theory states that two or more persons are needed, and that the double bind experience has to be repeated (not just a single incident). For the classic model, there must be a primary negative injunction (you better not do such and such), with the threat of punishment to back it up. Then there is a second injunction, one which conflicts with the first one (at a more abstract level), and, like the first, will be enforced by punishment (you had better darn well do such and such). A third negative injunction prevents the person from escaping the situation, a logical and reasonable response to the double bind—hence, he or she is forced to exist in a contradictory, confusing interpersonal environment, there's no running away. You are damned if you do and damned if you don't, and you can't avoid one response or the other. After an individual regularly encounters lots of double binds in his or her world, it is not even necessary to have all of the above ingredients to set off the confusion. One or two of the three injunctions can trigger it. The humorous example of this kind of interaction is depicted in Dan Greenberg's book, _How To Be A Jewish Mother_. (Greenberg is clear that any mother can be a "Jewish Mother") He describes the young man who finds two brand new shirts on his dresser one day. Not knowing for sure what to do with them, since he wasn't told they were his, he left them alone for awhile. Then one day he gets up his courage, puts one on and goes downstairs, where his mother says, "What's the matter? Didn't you like the other one?"

Power Structure

In many families, the power structure is not what it appears to be on the surface. For example, the father may look like he is in charge, but the mother may make all the rules in the household. The mother may command through the father, or vice versa. Frequently an out of control kid is the one who is calling the shots in the family, sometimes because no one wants to start the uproar that always occurs when this person does not get his or her way. People walk on eggshells when that individual is in the house. Most healthy families have some kind of shared control between the adults in the household, and most children appreciate the adults taking control, even though they may regularly complain when they don't get what they want. At a basic emotional level, there is a sense of relief and a feeling of safety when adults take charge, because kids know that they don't have what it takes to be in control. The healthy family is generally consistent and has clearly articulated limits. Consistency is important so kids know just what to expect, what they can count on. Limit setting is important because kids need to know just how far they can go before they get into trouble. They need to have the opportunity for "freedom", but within clear boundaries. When they learn this in the family, they have a better chance of making it successfully outside the family, in school and in the larger society.

Decision-making

This is related to the power structure, in that the power structure is what sets up the decision-making process. In some families, the individuals with the power make the decisions. In others, they delegate the decisions in various ways. For example, in some families, there is a democratic process in place. Everyone is considered a family member with some say in the family decisions that need to be made. Family conferences are made and there is a striving for consensus. The problem with a truly democratic process is that children, even those well into their teens, are not completely "mature" and ready to make all their own life decisions. If they were, they likely would not still be at home and living in their parents' household. Even democracies should have leaders, and the parents need to take that role. It is generally good to get the input of the kids as part of the decision making process, but it is important to let them know that the final decrees will always be made by the parents—like Harry Truman said, "The buck stops here." Again, when kids know that ultimately, the parents are in control, it is a comforting thought. It lends a sense of predictability and stability to their world. They need to be able to count on their parents to watch over them and keep them safe.

Emotional Stability

Just like individuals, families vary as to how they are functioning emotionally, from calm and pleasant to tense and distraught. As suggested above, when someone is out of control in the family, it causes a lot of turmoil and distress among the other family members. Being out of control may be the result of oppositional or antisocial behavior; it may be because of mental or physical illness; or it may be because of transient or situational problems confronting the family. It is important to address these issues quickly, because in a system such as the family, issues that weaken one aspect of family life tend to leak over into other areas. Family systems are like hydraulic systems; a leak in one "part" affects the "whole" system.

Problem Solving

Dealing with the various family members and with how they as individuals (as well as the family as a whole) deal with influences outside the family requires the solving of problems. Even for functional, "healthy" families, life is not without its challenges. The system that tries to solve all problems from the top is one which will soon find the top person being worn out and not able to do a good job in other areas. Usually the most effective way for any system to solve problems is to delegate some of the tasks to the people who do them best, and then to give them credit when jobs are well done. Families are not much different. For the parents to try to solve all the problems in the family without the input and help from other family members is like a pitcher on a baseball team trying to solve the problems in the outfield by trying to pitch a perfect game—it is possible, but not time after time.

Most parents with more than one child will soon find out that each individual child tends to respond best to an approach specific to that child (and different from the approaches used for other children). One child may respond best to an authoritarian and firm approach. Another may wilt in the same situation, but bloom with a more encouraging and inviting attitude. Generally, it is a good idea not to try to take exactly the same approach with everyone, and it is a good idea to let everyone know, that

76

the variation is on purpose and that is how it will be. Explain that you will approach each family member in the manner that fits him or her best, taking into consideration such things as individual personalities and age, and that you will try to be as fair as you can be. This kind of open communication reduces the possibility of complaints later about inconsistency.

Interdependency

In a family system, family members tend to be interdependent upon one another. Sometimes it is subtle, sometimes not. Each parent soon learns what they do best and what the other does best and often, without thinking about it, each does what they do best without checking with the other. For example, one parent usually falls into being the bill payer, at first through choice, and then out of habit. Another may mow the grass when it needs it. Some chores are alternated, depending on what the other is doing. Kids are often expected to do some of the household chores. It is probably best to alternate those, so one kid does not see himself or herself strictly as the dishwasher, hedge trimmer or garbage carrier. Also as kids get older they can handle more and more, and the chores and household jobs that they do should reflect, to some extent, their increasing abilities to take on more complex tasks. A smooth running family, through dividing up all the various tasks required to keep the household going, sets up a complex web of interdependency which sustains the smoothness.

Family Values

Each system has values, and family systems are no exception. These values are often tied in to that family's specific culture, including its religious and ethnic aspects. In a family there are two people who come together, and then (usually) have kids who will in turn develop their own family systems. Each of these individuals was raised in his or her own system, bringing their own unique heritage. One person may have been from a family where divorce occurred. The other may have come from a family where divorce is the last thing that would have been allowed. So what happens when the marriage gets rocky?—a lot depends on the inculcation of values from the original family structures. Issues that come up for teens as the family progresses will be viewed differently in different families. Issues such as teen sex and pregnancy, homosexuality, academic progress, athletics, discipline, drug abuse, and interfaith dating will be dealt with differently in various family systems.

Breaking from the System or the Culture

When an individual breaks from a culture or from a system, it may be a conscious decision to do so, or it may be a circumstance that evolves gradually (either by chance or by necessity). Sometimes practicality enters and causes some disruption. A common example of this is seen when a family member is transferred by his or her company to a new location, away from extended family and from friends. The need is there, because job opportunities are limited, and a family needs to be fed, housed and clothed. Such a disruption may immerse the family into another subculture, mixing traditions, and geographic distance may not allow very frequent contact with the old traditions and patterns. Some are carried on, but others are altered. Children connect with other children at schools and parents meet other parents. New patterns are established. We see that separation and distance can play a part, pragmatics plays a part, and mixing in with other cultures and traditions can play a part.

Sometimes there is a conscious decision on the part of individuals to break away from some of the older traditions. It may be rebellion; it may be the result of education or a change in thinking about some subject; it may be the result of a religious experience. Whatever the cause, people do sometimes make the decision to consciously change the patterns of their lives, and begin to alter the habits and choices of much of their upbringing.

Family Membership

In centuries past the concept of family was important for reasons that are rarely relevant to life in the 21st century. Families were often counted on for such important functions as protection from enemies, security in old age, and help on the farm or in the business. In the present day, some families still tend to live and work in the same general area, but our society is much more mobile—much of the time people move away from their extended families, drawn to other towns or states by education, work, climate or just desire for change. Yet most of us are still aware of our uncles, aunts, cousins and grandparents and how we are connected. At the same time, perhaps because of the distances that often occurs between blood relatives, families frequently "adopt" close friends as though they were family members. I remember as a kid having an "Uncle Andy" who was not really an uncle, but who was frequently at our house, made himself at home, put the coffee on if my parents were not yet out of bed, and might even bake biscuits before we all got up. His wife was ill at the time, and lived in a Sanatorium for people with tuberculosis, so we "adopted" him. When we moved to Oregon from Wisconsin, our kids had no grandparents close by, and we became friends with an elderly couple across the street. She had tea parties with our daughter and her friends, and they became surrogate grandparents. We still exchange gifts at Christmas and birthdays, even after the kids are grown.

Divorce

What happens when a family gets blown apart? First of all, there are no easy answers in divorce. It is a traumatic event for some (or all) no matter how well it is done, yet about half of U.S. families end in divorce. It is no longer an uncommon occurrence in our culture. People no longer blindly accept the old adage, "You made your bed, so now you have to sleep in it." If a marriage is bad, sometimes it is best for the partners and for the kids to end it so that more emotional trauma does not occur. In the event of divorce, "damage control" is important in several areas:

1) Kids often will blame themselves for the split-up of their parents. They need reassurance that they are not the cause of the divorce, that it was an adult decision, and also that they were not expected to "fix" the relationship of the two adults.

2) In virtually all breakups, significant contact with the absent parent is extremely important—the adults need to arrange

for continuity of both parental relationships with the kids, assuming it is safe for them.

3) Parents should not be putting down the other parent in front of the kids, in spite of their own anger and their own feelings or assessment of the situation and its causes.

4) Kids should not be used as messengers from one parent to another. As much as possible, they should be kept out of the "war zone".

5) If parents use the kids to get back at one another (withholding visitation, not being available for phone calls, etc.) it is emotionally destructive for the children.

6) Life must go on as "normally" as possible for the kids. If visitation schedules are set up, they should be structured around the kids' schedules for school and extracurricular activities, not those of the parents.

7) There will be grieving, and grief is an emotional condition that takes some time to dissipate. Kids should not be expected to "just get over it"—upset feelings from the loss of the presence of one of the parents will take time to dissipate. This may take awhile for some kids who may tend to blame one parent or the other for the breakup.

8) If a new partner enters into the picture, there will likely be resentment, no matter how nice a person he or she is. Do not expect that new parental figure to immediately become a regular disciplinarian because it probably won't work very well. An extended length of time as part of the family and a lot of groundwork (especially in the area of trust) is usually required before children can comfortably accept the newcomer in a role of authority.

9) Don't assume that because a kid is acting very "mature" and doesn't talk about the divorce much, that it isn't affecting him/her. Count on the fact that it is. Occasionally kids are relieved that their parents divorced, because there is less fight-

ing and emotional strain, but there is usually still a sense of loss as well.

In most cases, a big problem with divorce is that the children and their needs and feelings are considered last. The marriage partners are usually very hurt, frightened, and/or angry. In the early stages of divorce, they are often acting more like children than adults in charge of children. They tend to maneuver for position, emotional and sometimes financial, and custody of the kids is often a bargaining chip for other concessions. Children may be played off one another or off the parents. The result for kids, including teenagers, is often a sense of abandonment, of loss, of mixed loyalties, of disruption, and of pain. For a lot of kids, they experience a buildup of negative emotions, especially anger and depression. The child is often left to live with one parent who not only is dealing with the emotional upheaval of divorce but now is stressed with having to raise the kids alone. It is generally easier for the child to take his anger out on this custodial, "safe" parent, though the anger may really be at the absent one. If that absent parent is confronted at the next opportunity, the fear is that that parent will abandon the child even more. It's a tough situation for many kids, and it can take months or even years before the pain and problems fade.

Single parenting can be a very difficult job. There is no letup and less opportunity to have someone spell you. Sometimes friends will help out, but the feeling is always there that some reciprocity is in order. One feels the need to pay back in kind, and money can be an issue as well. Many single parents end up finding another partner, and often this is where families really get complicated. When a potential new spouse enters the picture, things tend to heat up. Not only does it destroy any reconciliation fantasies the children may have been harboring, but they also may perceive a transfer of love and attention away from them to this "intruder", a "stranger". They often are aggravated by the physical/romantic connecting of the adults, either witnessed or presumed. Though they know that their parents certainly must have been physical to the point of sexual congress, it was always that way from the beginning, and thus it was o.k. Most kids just don't think much about their parents' romantic/sex life, or when they do it is more on an intellectual level, not an emotional one. When kids see their divorced parent in what is obviously becoming a romantic relationship (and maybe a sexual one), they may get very upset. This is often true for the parent who has left the home as well as the custodial parent. For some reason, even if it is o.k. to leave, when that parent becomes interested in someone else, strong negative feelings often follow. Kids just find it hard to accept it when either of their parents have adult-adult romantic relationships with anyone other than one another. Then if you take that scenario to the new romantic partner and to his or her ex and kids, the potential for fireworks increases dramatically.

Blended families (reconstituted families, stepfamilies, bi-nuclear families) can become quite well-knit and can function well together, but kids do much better if they think that they are participating in the healing process. It is probably best not to expect them to accept the newcomers in roles that are very different from what they were experiencing shortly before the families were officially blended. Ease them into the new situation nice and slowly. Be invitational when you can. Do not expect that the new parent figure will be taking anyone's place, but instead adding something novel and positive to the family structure, and as mentioned above, don't expect the new parent to become the primary disciplinarian.

Here are some interesting facts about blended families:

1) In 1990, Dr. Ken Magid reported that the number of stepfamilies was increasing by 1300 each day, making 35 million stepfamilies in the US as of 1990, with another 35 million living in non-married "pseudo stepfamily" relationships, bringing the total of blended families to 70 million.

2) According to Dr. Emily Visher, co-founder of the Stepfamily Association of California, if one considers a nuclear family with two parents, two children and four grandparents, there is a potential network of 247 different combinations of relatives. If

one parent remarries a new partner with 3 children, 136 pairs and 131,054 combinations of relationships can result. If a divorced man with two children marries a widow with one child and his former wife marries a man who has three children by a former marriage, the result is three families and six children or 253 pairs and 8,388,584 combinations. Is it any wonder that children can find themselves in a constant state of adaptation, feeling overwhelmed, feeling divided loyalties, and feeling confused?

3) Among the changes kids go through are the feelings of loss of one parent (or sometimes both if the residing parent is thoroughly engaged in another relationship), sometimes a change in place of residence, schools, neighborhood and friends, and always some changes in their relationships with their parents. In addition there are new relationships to be established and defined with step-parents and there may be stepsiblings also to contend with. It is important to be realistic. Such a blend does not come together quickly or easily. Putting together a new family with its own beliefs, rituals, values, communication patterns, power structure, etc., out of two (or more) previous families with their own unique definitions in all these areas, gathered from previous generational "hand-me-downs", creates a multitude of rituals, values, and so on, for the kids to sort through and absorb in the formation of a new stepfamily. It is no wonder that many kids, especially teenagers who are about to leave the nest soon anyway, opt out of trying to accommodate this new creation. Parents can only be patient, try hard to include the kids all through the process of blending, keep order in the family, and try to be understanding and accommodating to the kids' needs—and remember, sometimes it works out fine.

Other Significant Family Changes

There are numerous common events or situations, other than those touched on above, that potentially can cause considerable changes in families. Discussed below are a few of the most important ones.

Adoption: Adopting a child can significantly alter a family constellation, as much or even more than a natural child entering a family system. And with the adoption of an older child, there is often not the same kind of bonding that occurs as with a brand new infant. Adoptees often bring with them issues of abandonment, even if they are adopted at a relatively early age. Kids often want to have a sense of their biological roots. There are medical history issues. There can be problems with other children feeling displaced, though that could occur with a birth into the family as well. With pregnancy, there is a nine month wait and period to accustom the family both psychologically and visibly to the coming of another child. With adoption, it often feels more sudden than that. However, announcements, planning, and discussion, all aid in a positive family preparation for the newcomer.

In the teen years, when the struggle for identity comes into full swing, the child who has been adopted can become intensely interested in his or her biological roots. As discussed at length in Chapter II, adolescence is a time when one wants to really know and understand oneself. Part of finding one's direction for adult life is to know where one comes from. A firm grounding in the culture of the adoptive family helps the individual kid to know more thoroughly who he or she is, but a sense of biological roots is also reassuring to some kids, both from a medical as well as a psychological vantage point. It is important for the adoptive parents not to become threatened by such a need. It does not carry with it a sense of disrespect or displacement, and surprisingly, sometimes your support and help for a bio-parental search will further cement the bonds between kids and their adoptive families.

Illness: Whenever any family member becomes ill, it impacts on the family system, and very significantly if the illness is severe, chronic or terminal. A lot of energy goes into the care of an ill member, and it shifts the emphasis of the family so that the normal comings and goings of the rest of the family get less focus. The encouragement one member may commonly get before the weekend game can get lost. The excellent grade on the exam may seem to be ignored. If it is a parent that is ill, it is especially difficult to pick up the slack; if it is a child, the focus of the family may seem to track that child and not others. Having a severely ill child can be exhausting, but it is important to remember that the whole family suffers. It is important to keep track of what all the other family members are doing as well.

Hospitalization: In addition to illness, hospitalization takes an added toll. The trips back and forth to visit, yet the need to attend to those at home, requires increased attention and expends a lot of energy. It is exhausting, especially if it has to go on for an extended time. Parents may need to accept the help of those friends or extended family who are willing to pitch in to give a hand, and if you need to and can afford it, consider hiring some help.

Death: Whether it is expected or not, whether it is in immediate or extended family, death is a painful thing to deal with. Sometimes it is a relief, but it still comes as a loss. If it is in the immediate family, it leaves a gaping hole. It is important to grieve, and to let others do so at their own pace. People deal with their grief differently; some with irritability, some with tears, some with outright anger, and some with withdrawal. Teens may have their first taste of death in a family member or in a friend. Understand that this may be the first real sense of their own mortality and they may be scared. It may be a time when a clergyman can be very helpful to the family.

Moving: Always a stress to kids, and especially teenagers, is the thought of moving from their neighborhood, from their town, from their school, or from their friends. Whether this occurs because of a divorce, a job change, an eviction, or whatever, it is worth the time to listen to your kid's distress and to try to be supportive about the emotional stresses of change as much as you can. Work on identifying and then emphasizing the positives.

Financial stress: Parents tend to be more stressed by financial considerations than do kids. Nonetheless, when parents are stressed, the overall mood and tone tend to overflow and be picked up by other family members. Remember, generally kids recognize that they have a shot at making a living of their own at some time in the future. They usually are not as stressed about lack of money as their parents; they are used to being poor. However, some fallout from financial stress, such as being forced to move, can have a much more disturbing effect on kids.

War and Terrorism: The bombings of the World Trade Center towers and the Pentagon have indicated that the United States is not impervious to military attack. Random shootings as we have too often seen in the news make similar impacts. Events such as these, especially when close to home, often have a profound effect on the adults of the family. Add the distress seen in parents to the inevitable media coverage of the horrors of war and terrorism, and even relatively young children may be disturbed by it all. Everyone in the family reacts to this kind of tension—it undermines feeling safe and secure. Families that pull together through extended time together and talking about the disturbing events generally get through it with the least amount of enduring trauma to the family unit and its individual members. Indeed, sometimes through experiencing and overcoming the effects of such tragedies comes increased bonding and a strengthening of the sense of family.

Concepts Of Discipline

People have viewed discipline in many ways over the years. "Spare the rod and spoil the child" is one very well known point of view. A radically different viewpoint is expressed in the phrase, "Crack the shell and the egg spills out." Teenagers who are engaged in sports will come up against coaches who constantly ride them and regularly spew out negative commentary when mistakes are made. Others will experience coaches who are encouraging, who give a lot of praise for a job well done, but who push the athlete to stretch oneself to perform better. Generally, of these two types, the coaches that are remembered as the best teachers and the ones who inspired them the most, are those who were regularly positive and encouraging, while pushing them to stretch their limits and capabilities. Both types of discipline may work, at least to some extent, but which is the most effective and efficient? The old idea that people should not be praised for things that they were supposed to do anyway, doesn't really encourage effort. Studies have shown that "intermittent positive reinforcement" is the most effective way to encourage a particular behavior, and we want to encourage certain behaviors until the social reinforcement that they get for doing those behaviors continues to keep them going without our intervention. Intermittent positive reinforcement means that there is a positive thing that happens every once in a while—enough that it keeps us going to try to get that response. A good example is the one-armed bandit or slot machine. It only pays off every once in a while, but just enough to keep people putting coins into the machine in hopes of hitting the jackpot. Another is the father who decides to take the kids fishing or to the beach every so often, when he feels that they have done a great job for a period of time with their chores. It encourages the kids to keep up the good work in hopes of some more fun times with dad.

Physical discipline is usually not a good idea. At some level, it is important that kids know that their parents may be pushed to the limit, where it could be a possibility, but ultimately, it models aggression to solve problems, and that is rarely a good idea. At the same time, it is important to set limits and boundaries, and to consistently follow through with consequences for behavior. If kids do not see their parents or other adults as being in control, it can be frightening, and kids will often push the limits to the point where they see that adults around them finally take control, and then they will push them again to make sure that those adults maintain that control.

The Teen In All This

Family relationships in general are very complex, and in a teen's world, one which is complicated by school and peer issues, sports, concerns about identity and the discovery of who one is and where one is headed, the emergence of sexuality, and the overbearing presence in our day and age of the drug scene, the further complication of family problems just adds fuel to the fire. Also, when difficulties occur for one of the parents or kids, it tends to impact the whole family system so that outside help is sometimes needed. There are counselors, social workers, psychologists and psychiatrists who are very experienced in helping families sort out difficulties which may arise in marriages, school problems, behavior problems, drug and alcohol abuse, mental health problems, identity problems, difficulties with peers, and so on. Getting in touch with your local medical society, psychological association, or primary care physician may be the means to getting to someone who can be helpful to the whole family system.

Legal issues that may arise:
Most states in the U.S. recognize the legal age of its citizens as 18 years. Prior to the age of 18, most states also hold parents responsible for actions performed by their kids. Thus, we need to be vigilant about what our kids are up to, as much as we are able. There are bad decisions that kids can make that might make us liable for damage or harm done. There are some things that are particularly prone to be used in ways that, in spite of how good our kids are, are liable to be used with poor judgment. Some of these are automobiles, guns, prescription drugs and alcohol, and in states where cannabis is legal, marijuana. These are all things that are often accessible at home, and it is very important that they are all carefully monitored, and hopefully inaccessible, when monitoring adults are not around. It is important that we recognize our liability in what our kids do, in addition to what difficulties our kids can get into, as well as potential harm accidentally done.

Another family liability issue can be the "attractive nuisance". Things such as swimming pools, unemptied wading pools, tree houses, tools not put away, hoses not coiled, are potentially accidents waiting to happen. Care must be taken to warn of risks and to make hazards unaccessible.

Clearly a litany of potential legal issues is not possible in this book, but parents should be aware of some of them, and if in need of legal counsel and not knowing where to start, one place to go is to one's local bar association for help in selecting appropriate legal counsel.

Pearls For Parents:

There are no cookbook recipes for raising kids. Our complex society and world has evolved to the point where it takes not only patience, perseverance and wisdom to raise our teenage kids, but also some good luck. Sometimes the thing that families can count on the most to be certain that they connect together regularly is always having some meals together in the busy hustle and bustle of daily living. For this reason, we are including the Vergamini spaghetti recipe in this chapter to do our part to encourage you to have at least one or two good meals together a week. Mrs. Ruth Vergamini used to open the windows when she made the sauce, "so all the neighbors would get jealous". It will bring the kids home, and the sauce makes enough so that when they drag their friends along, there will be plenty of food.

Vergamini Spaghetti Sauce
from the Kitchen of Judy and Jerry Vergamini

Warning: steel pots tend to burn in hot spots. Use aluminum or coated cookware. Use a large pot.

Allow for gathering of ingredients, cleaning/rinsing your choice of meats, getting rid of small bones, pouring light cooking oil (Wesson or Olive or Canola oil on bottom of pot to brown the meats prior to opening cans of tomato sauce and tomato paste and pouring an equal amount of water per can of tomato sauce and can of paste into cooking pot. Watch sauce for low boil. Then turn to low simmer, pour off visible extra oils, stir and add spices and continue to gently stir throughout the cooking time. Add any spices throughout cooking time, according to your preferences. Stir sauce at intervals. Maintain cooking for six to eight hours. Check that meats are cooked to soft degree and not sticking to bottom of pot. Do not cook at high heat after low boil has been reached. In separate pots, cook your choice of pastas. We cook rigatoni and spaghetti and serve separately, with sauce, according to choice. Meats are also served in separate bowls to allow people to choose meats and pasta as is desired.

Ingredients:
Whole Chicken Fryer, cut up, small bones removed, plus, at least, six to twelve more parts, such as, thighs and/or breasts
Spare ribs or beef short ribs or country short ribs - Remove any membranes
Enough light oil to lightly cover bottom of pot, TO KEEP MEATS FROM BURNING
One can of water per empty can of tomato paste and tomato sauce, using cans for measurement
Four to six 15 ounce cans of Tomato Sauce
Eight Twelve ounce cans of Tomato Paste
Two cans of sliced tomato pieces
10 teaspoons of Oregano (flat teaspoon of ground Oregano or slightly heaping teaspoon if leaves). We prefer ground Oregano.
4 teaspoons of ground Parsley
4-6 teaspoons Sweet Basil Leaves. Remove Leaves at end of cooking time!!
Two teaspoons of Rosemary
Five scant (level) teaspoons of Garlic Powder- Do not increase garlic powder, if recipe is increased, keep the same amount of garlic powder-5 level teaspoons!
4 teaspoons of salt
2 teaspoons of Pepper
6-7 teaspoons of Sugar (or equivalent of Sugar Twin or 2-3 packages of false sugar)
2-3 teaspoons of Italian Seasoning
Small or sliced Mushrooms, Optional, Mild Seasoning of mushrooms can be done in separate pan and added to sauce close to end of cooking time or served separately
> Salad and Garlic Bread are desirable additions to the meal
> Parmesan Cheese is often enjoyed with the meal
> Sauce can be frozen with or without meats

ENJOY!

A NICE DESSERT to have in an evening with a glass of milk is a great chocolate cake that Mrs. Ruth Vergamini used to make from scratch—it was called WACKY CAKE.

Wacky Cake Ingredients:

1 and 1/2 cups cake flour
1 teaspoon baking soda
1 cup sugar
1/2 teaspoon salt
3 tablespoons cocoa (unsweetened)
6 tablespoons cooking oil
1 tablespoon vinegar
1 teaspoon vanilla
1 cup cold water

Sift flour, sugar, cocoa, baking soda and salt together into an ungreased baking dish.

Punch 3 holes of graduated sizes into the mixture. In the largest hole, pour cooking oil. Pour vinegar in the medium hole and vanilla into the smallest one. Cover with one cup cold water. Stir well with a fork and bake right in the mixing dish for 25 minutes at 350 degrees.

Frost this cake right in the pan, because the cake is so soft that it will break if attempted to be removed in one piece.

Resources:

Classic Movies:

"The Accidental Tourist" (William Hurt, Gena Davis)

"Crimes of The Heart" (Jessica Lange,
Sissy Spacek, Diane Keaton)

"The Great Santini" (Robert Duvall)

"Home For The Holidays" (Holly Hunter)

"Ordinary People" (Tim Hutton, Mary Tyler
Moore, Donald Sutherland, Judd Hirsh)

"On Golden Pond" (Henry Fonda,
Katherine Hepburn, Jane Fonda)

"Terms of Endearment" (Jack Nicholson, Shirley MacLaine,
John Lithglow, Debra Winger, Jeff Daniels, Danny DeVito)

"The Man Without a Face" (Mel Gibson)

"This Boy's Life" (Robert DeNiro)

"What's Eating Gilbert Grape?" (Johnny
Depp, Mary Steenburgen)

Books:

The Human Comedy by William Saroyan

My Name is Aram by William Saroyan

Chapter 5
PEER RELATIONSHIPS

"All for one, and one for all."
— **Alexander Dumas The Three Musketeers**

The three major areas that we look at when determining how a child or teen is doing in his life, are family, school and peers. Relationships with peers are one of the main building blocks to forming warm and loving relationships with others. It is a cornerstone of building intimacy. This is not to say we are talking about sexual intimacy alone, but the ability to be accepting of others for who they are, and to form warm, lasting friendships, which, hopefully, will evolve into the ability to form similar future spousal, family, and work relationships. Second only after families, the relationships with peers form the groundwork of learning to build trust, and sometimes when families are not sufficient to provide a good medium in which trust can grow, positive peer relationships will help. In the teen years, peer relationships are especially important.

If we relook at the **developmental stages of play** in children, we see that children first engage in parallel play, i.e., they do their own thing alongside other children who are doing their own thing. Eventually the other child will want what the first child has, and the tug of war begins. Adults have to intervene at first, but eventually the children begin to learn cooperative play, or taking turns, or learning to wait and to use toys when the other is done. Eventually in addition to being cooperative, the play becomes more interactive, with play involving the active imagination of both children, or groups of children. As very young children, sex differences don't seem to make a lot of difference, unless taught differently. As they get older and into pre-adolescence, they tend to group off into males and females, into what we might call homosocial groupings. Preteens and early teens tend to hang out with members of the same sex, with similar interests, such as sports, music, games, and so on. Even though they may have an interest in the opposite sex, they tend to hang out together with others of the same sex. Eventually the groupings get together and groups of boys spend time with groups of girls, or groups of boys will congregate around a particularly attractive girl, who may be flattered by the attention. It is usually the older adolescent who will begin to break off from the group part of the time, to put his attention to a particular partner of the opposite sex. Interestingly this may be to the chagrin of the remaining part of the group. They see the beginning of the old gang breaking up. However as one after another break off into pairing, or partnering up with someone of the opposite sex, others usually follow the lead. Such pairing at this early stage is often brief or short-lived, but nevertheless, it is quite intense. So called "Puppy Love" is not to be scoffed at, since, regardless of the age, it is emotionally very real.

What are some of the **specific issues** that kids deal with among their peers at this age?

Anomie is a state or condition characterized by a breakdown or absence of social norms or values. It comes from the Greek word for lawlessness. We see many kids struggling with what the norms are for their peer group. Are they the same as those of the adults around them? Often not. We see it foremost in their dress, then in their music, in their language, and certainly in their protests. Causes are important to teens, just as they are to adults, yet causes help teens to cement their values and ideals and may give them future direction. When we can, we need to help them to find paths short of extremes to further their causes.

Parental influence is another important issue for teens. The impact of modeling on teens cannot be underestimated. Good example goes a long way, even when kids are in the process of purposefully ignoring it for the purpose of their own autonomy. I have often said to parents that I do not care what a kid thinks of me at age 13 to 17 as much as I care what the kid thinks of me at age 23-27. It is important for the kid to know where we stand on minor issues as well as major ones, and it is also important for them to know that sometimes we have not thought out an issue yet, in order to be able to form an opinion about it. In other words, it is important for kids to see us as human and capable of error, so that they can learn from us how we deal with our mistakes, because they know we do make them, whether we let on about it or not.

Learning Other-Directedness is a task important to teens and found in family relationships as well as through peer inter-action. There is nothing like peer pressure to make one aware of what others need from you. It makes us adults aware of the power of peer pressure, especially when we see early teens dressing alike, listening to the same music, using the same terminology and language, and walking the same gait. Yet peer pressure can go both ways, and it is important to present a model for our kids to fit in among their peers while making decisions that are individual and can be directed toward the common good of others as well as themselves and their cohort.

Street kids or kids who have decided to step out of their parental homes for shorter or longer periods of time and live with "friends" on the street are commonplace. The epitome of "anomie", these kids may be punkers, sporting similar uniforms of studded black clothes, heavy black boots, shaved heads, studded collars, tatoos, or spiked mohawks, or hippie wannabes with multicolored tie-dyed clothes and dreadlocks or carefully casual oversize baggy jeans and sweaters. Some of these kids live on the streets out of necessity, having been kicked out of parental homes, perhaps because they refused to follow rules or expectations. Some choose to live this way for short periods, to be with friends, returning home periodically for a warm bed and good food (three hots and a cot).

The dangers of this kind of existence is often more clear to adults than to the kids. Sexual assault is not uncommon. Risk of sexually transmitted disease is present. Other illnesses are a risk, with poor nutrition, exposure to contagious diseases, and poor hygiene. Other types of physical assault can be imminent. Unfortunately, the authorities cannot do much these days to help parents in the dilemma of pulling their kids off the streets. The people who have made the laws do not always seem to have a good grasp on adolescent development, and the laws are interpreted to assume that teens are little adults, or people who should be treated equally as adults, yet their life experience is not that of adults, nor often is their judgment. Being a runaway is considered a "status offense" in most states. Paradoxically, kids are allowed to live as though they were adults, until they commit a more significant crime. Then the parents are held responsible and have to pay fines and damages; yet the law often cannot come to the aid of parents prior to bigger trouble.

What can parents do? Be invitational to these kids when you can, but not to the point of inviting chaos back into the family. Within the boundaries of civility and courtesy among all family members, let them know that you care about them, but to return, even for short periods, there are limits to behaviors, as well as some expectations. The concept of "room-mate rules" is a good one. Basically what this means is that living with other people means needing to get along like good room-mates, respecting the needs and rights of others. If you cannot do that, you cannot live here. You cannot be coming and going only as you choose (crashing and eating) without predictability for others and using the goods of others as you choose. You're not entitled to that. If you don't want to go along with those expectations, we change the locks and take our chances that you will be OK. If we think you will not be safe, we'll call the Department of Human Services or the police.

Unfortunately, many kids will push the limits to see how far they can go. Often they secretly wish that someone would place limits on their behavior, but at another level, they want to experience the opportunity to be on their own and to have autonomy, much like the two year old, who says, "No!"

Gangs are a big issue for teens these days, whether one belongs, wants to belong, or has to watch out for those who do belong. Gangs can be considered to be a loosely organized group of individuals who collaborate together for social, economic or safety reasons. They have been around for a long time. Pirates were early gang members. Various bands of brigands were others. Gangs are not necessarily illegal, but a lot of the gangs today, especially youthful gangs, use illegal activities to finance gang activities or to enhance their reputation on the streets. Gangs usually have a leader or group of leaders who issue the orders and benefit from the gang's activities. Gangs today may wear "colors", certain types of clothing, tatoos, brands, or otherwise may imprint their gang's logo or identifying marks on their bodies. They may wear certain hairstyles, use hand signals, or spray graffiti on walls, street signs, dumpsters, school property, etc. Graffiti is like a newspaper or bulletin board for the gang's communication and is commonly used to send messages, mark territories, warn other gang members, boast about deeds, etc.

There are a number of reasons why kids join or form into gangs. One is a sense of **identity**, a sense of being someone special. Another is a sense of **belonging**, to a specific group. A third is for a sense of safety or protection from other predatory individuals or gangs. A kid looking for a purpose may find something to belong to in a gang with a reputation. The interaction of members, listening to one another's problems, and sharing the difficulties of today's teens can all be drawing cards to belonging to a gang. The **recognition** of belonging to such a group as something special is another reason to join. The **discipline** of the gang is a draw for many. The fact that, once in a gang, the participants (or "bangers") are told that there is no way out, means a lifetime of fealty to the group that is backed up by the group. A sense of **loyalty** or even **love** is established, and is another draw to kids to belong. Then there is the **money**. A lot of neighborhood gangs were mainly social in nature until meth and crack cocaine became available on the streets. Then the enterprise became lucrative. Money became a big factor and gangs vied for territory where they could make big money. What used to settled with fists now became settled with lead. Eventually many kids joined gangs because of **intimidation or continued threats and harrassment** by the gang. It might have been considered to be less dangerous to belong than not to belong. Yet, once in, the banger must conform to the rules and culture of the gang.

To understand the gang mentality, one must have a sense of its culture. The three "R's" of gang culture are: **Reputation, Respect** and **Retaliation (or Revenge).**

Rep or reputation extends not only to the individual but to the entire group. Status or rank in the gang depends on the amount of "juice" based largely on one's reputation.

Respect is needed for not only the individual, but also for the group, its territory, family, or anything else thought to deserve it by the group. Included in the respect one has for one's own group is often the requirement that one have <u>disrespect</u> for another group or gang. Failure to "dis" another gang may be perceived as a "dis" to his own group and may be punished ("beaten down") by his own.

Retaliation—In gang culture, no challenge can respectfully go unanswered. Drive-by shootings and other violent confrontations may often follow an event that was considered a "dis". Such activities may come from the result of an infringement on territory, a bad drug deal, a rival gang member displaying a gang sign, "tagging" (graffiti) in the wrong territory or a confrontation between a group of one gang and a member of another, resulting in the single person going to get reinforcements.

One should keep in mind that street gangs are very fluid in nature, and while it may be very easy at times to develop information about them, the nature of the gangs is such that the events occur or the information changes, before it can be used to much advantage to the law enforcement authorities, until after the fact.

What should parents or others in authority look for in kids in regard to gang activity?

1) The kid who admits to gang activity.

2) The kid who is obsessed with one particular color or type of clothing or who insists on wearing one type of logo over another.

3) The kid who wears excessive jewelry with distinctive designs and may wear it only on one side of his body.

4) The kid who is obsessed with gangster-influenced music, movies or videos to the point

5) The kid who withdraws from his family with an accompanying change in manner and general demeanor.

6) The kid who associates with undesirables and breaks parental rules regularly.

7) The kid who develops an inordinate sense of privacy and secrecy and may even rearrange his room to create more privacy.

8) The kid who uses hand signs with friends and practices them at home.

9) The kid with physical injury who lies about how it happened.

10) The kid who has peculiar drawings or language on school books or as tatoos or brands.

11) The kid who has unexplained cash or goods like clothing or jewelry, etc.

12) The kid who may be using alcohol or drugs with an attitude change.

> Not each of these signs alone depict gang activity, but they should be warning signs for parents and others to look further, and if a number of these warning signs are present, be very suspicious.

What should parents warn their kids about in regard to gangs?

1) Not to associate with gang members or gang "wannabes" or "gonnabes".

2) Not to identify or communicate with gangs.

3) Not to hang out with where gangs congregate or near there.

4) Not to wear gang-related clothes or initialed clothing where gangs are known to hang out or pass through.

5) Not to use gang-related lingo, especially in malls, concerts or sporting events

6) Not to attend any function or party sponsored by a gang

7) Not to participate in any graffiti activity or hang out where there is graffiti.

8) Not to use any gang sign or finger or sign language in a public place.

Alternatives to gangs and the streets:

Kids tend to gravitate toward gangs and the streets for a sense of belonging and a sense of intimacy and closeness or friendship with their peers. If we can find other sources to fill these needs, we are in business. Most kids in their teen years are energetic and are coming into their own in terms of conceptualizing about the inconsistencies and injustices in the adult world around them. Most of the kids who hit the streets or reach out to gangs are looking for recognition or expressing their feelings about the hypocrisy they see around them. There needs to be alternatives to these options, and they are there if we can make them meaningful.

Sports have always been an avenue for excelling and for recognition among kids. Whether it is the big lumbering boy who can hold the center of the line on the football team, or the small skinny girl who can outrun and outmaneuver the other kids on the soccer field, there are enough sports in which kids can work hard to excel. In addition, sports offer an outlet for the natural energy and aggression so available in teens.

Music is another expressive outlet for teens. Whether the kid plays guitar in a garage rock band or cello in the school orchestra, music can be a significant force and means of achieving a sense of confidence and recognition.

For some kids more intellectually directed, there are numerous extracurricular clubs in schools which allow for expression and relationships to develop. Whether it is the Chess Club, the Spanish Club, or a Computer Club, the opportunity to meet others and gain recognition can be found.

Church or Synagogue Youth Groups offer an excellent opportunity to meet others with similar interests and to explore issues of the day in a positive and growthful manner. They usually combine a lot of fun with a mixture of light and serious talk about things that teens have to deal with on a day to day basis, as well as the opportunity to discuss some of the more momentous concerns of mankind over the centuries.

Jobs for kids are a touch of reality. They learn to be nice to people that they may not particularly like. They learn to be on time. They learn what it is to have to earn their money. They may learn what it is to be fired. They learn that jobs take time—away from play, away from friends, away from studies, away from just loafing, but jobs also give them money and to that extent some sense of freedom, and jobs can give them a sense of positive self-esteem. Jobs also give them experience to take to their next job. Also, the fact is (as my father once told me)—"When you're working, you're not spending."

Social Media:

These are computer or smart phone mediated tools that allow people, companies, or organizations to create, share, or exchange information, ideas, pictures and videos. Wikipedia spells out the complexity of these tools quite well for those who want a more comprehensive look. For our purposes, they are ubiquitous tools used by teens and adults alike to connect with others. They include texting, Facebook, Twitter, Snapchat, Instagram, Pinterest, Vine, WeChat, Flickr, You Tube, Tumblr, and whatever new app that has popped up between the writing of this information and the printing of this book. Access is easy, and whatever arrives on the internet can be considered to be available to others indefinitely in one form or another. The problem with social media is that our kids tend to use them freely and often without good judgment about consequences. Things that might be said to a close friend might be sent out for all to read. Photos of all types will likely be forwarded indefinitely, especially if they are the least bit risqué or confidential. Attempts to be accepted might result in personal information or photos to be sent out without realizing that they can be sent on beyond their expected audience.

Kids will do dumb things. It is part of growing up and learning from mistakes, but we do not want those dumb mistakes to be perpetuated in cyberspace. Thus, it is important that we have that talk with our kids before they start using computers and smart phones, much as we should have that talk about sexual behavior and consequences before they are at the point of no return. If they are going to be on Facebook, we need to be their friends on Facebook. If they use Twitter, we need to be followers on Twitter, and so on. They may kick about that, but we need to be able to see what they are up to and to be able to talk to them about it. There can also be legal implications to what our kids do, even on social media, but we will talk about that in another section of this book. Kids need to know about predators, and even though they may feel strong or invincible and smart, they are no match for some of the tools that predators use to gain their confidence and their hearts. We need to be clear about this and to teach them to avoid these temptations to get overly close and open with strangers on line. Predators are often quite skilled at "grooming" others that they see as vulnerable, particularly young teens. It is a slow and patient game that gradually builds friendliness and confidence in the "groomee" toward the groomer along with a sense of comfort. Kids need to be taught that there are bad people out there who will take advantage of them given the chance.

The National Association of Adult Survivors of Child Abuse (NAASCA) has a website that talks very specifically about the grooming process. It talks about the old urban legend of the frog, who, put into a pot of boiling water will naturally jump out; however if you put a frog into a pot of cool water and naturally turn up the heat, you'll end up with a boiled frog. Grooming is likewise a slow and deliberate process that can be for sexual advantage, for enhancing power or one's standing in a group, or for the perverse attempt to make others look bad to make oneself look better. It can often go hand in hand with bullying.

The grooming process as spelled out in the NAASCA website is particularly pertinent to teens that use cyberspace to explore relationships. It is described as a perversion of romantic courting – you find yourself interested in someone, find out everything you can about him/her, see how you might fit into each other's lives, spend lots of time together (often on line), and eventually become physically (or emotionally) intimate. According to one former FBI agent, Kenneth Lanning, there are five stages in the grooming process:

Identify the possible victim

Collect information about the possible victim

Fill a need in the possible victim

Lower inhibitions

Initiate abuse

Our teens need to know that there are predators out there who will take advantage of individuals who are struggling with self-esteem and a sense of loneliness, and though these people will initially show a sense of understanding and caring, that eventually they usually resort to shame and blame to keep their victims hooked in.

<u>Prevention of cyber abuse</u>: The first step is awareness. Modeling of appropriate physical and emotional boundaries is important. Talking about what is private and what is not and being open to talking about their concerns in an age-appropriate manner goes a long way. This is where, as quoted from "The Godfather" movie, (at least in cyberspace) you don't let anyone know what you are thinking outside the family.

Parents: Pick Your Fights!

Remember, there are **safety issues** and there are **irritation issues**. In regard to safety issues, hold the line. The answer is NO, but in regard to irritation issues that are not safety issues, the general rule is, "Do it somewhere else where I don't have to watch or hear it."

In our practices, we have both seen battles over hair, clothing, companions, school, and now more recently body piercing and tatoos. Some of these battles are not over the particulars, but where the limits are and who is in charge of how much. It is important to be clear about why, even though there is disagreement about whether it is reasonable. The kid doesn't have to agree with the reasonableness of the rules, but does need to know what they are and perhaps why the parent is laying it down, even if it is, "because your visual appearance at the dinner table is very distressing to me in such attire, making it hard for me to enjoy my meal", or "because you need a job to pay off your speeding ticket, and looking like that, no one will hire you, so you need to get a haircut, shave, and put on some clothes that are acceptable to a prospective employer."

Some things are not worth spending the energy to fight about. Remember, if you lay down the law about every little thing, then the kid does not learn to differentiate between the big things and the little things. If it is a matter of health or safety, be firm. If it is an irritant, think seriously about whether it is worth the fight.

Pearls For Parents:

1) Ambivalence in rules is trouble. Be clear about expectations. Kids will always come up with something that you haven't foreseen. If they do, and it needs a rule, make one.

2) Kids know intuitively by their teens what their parents expect, if the parents have been consistent and clear. Sometimes they will use parents as "the heavy" when they want to avoid something that will get them in trouble. They'll use the parents as an excuse about why they cannot go or be involved in whatever it is. Encourage that. Don't worry about what the other kids or their parents will think of you.

3) Don't be shy about calling other kids' parents to find out details about upcoming events, or clarification about various situations.

4) All decisions do not have to be made or even completed right away. If you are not sure, for example, what consequence to place on a particular behavior, tell the kid that you will think about it and/or discuss it with your spouse, and give the kid

a definitive answer later. It is fair to tell the kid approximately when you expect to be able to tell what it will be. If the kid fusses and wants an answer immediately, you might give a warning that if you have some time to think about it and talk it over, there is a better chance of a lesser sentence than if you have to give an answer immediately, and if you did give an answer, you could still change your mind after having time to think about it. The child should understand that if you get some time to cool off, consequences might be more palatable than if you have to decide while you are steamed about his/her behavior.

5) To the child who groans that you don't trust him/her because you want to follow on Twitter or friend on Facebook, the answer is simple: I am your parent, not your buddy. It is important that I know you are safe and not doing inappropriate things. All kids will do things that they regret afterwards; I have done so. My job is to do the best I can to prevent problems that you may later regret while giving you the opportunity to grow and make good choices. Trust is the result of good behavior over time, and the more I see of that, the more trust I will have in your judgment. The beginning of trust in this issue is when you accept that I am not trying to take over your life, but seeing that you trust me enough to know that, and by not making a fuss about my looking over your shoulder.

Be very clear that the old saying, "What happens in Vegas, stays in Vegas." does not apply to the internet. True – what happens on the internet, stays on the internet, but for anyone and everyone to read or watch, not just in Vegas, but in Omaha, Brooklyn, Chicago, San Francisco and the rest of the world. So be clear to your kids that if they post something, they had better hope that it is something that their parents, their minister, their teachers, and their grandparents and their potential boss (maybe even 10 years from now) would like to see there.

Resources:

Books:

Chicken Soup For The Teenage Soul by Jack Canfield,
  Mark Victor Hansen and Kimberly Kirberger, Health
  Communications, Inc., Deerfield Beach , Florida
  (www.hci-online.com)

Catcher In The Rye by J.D. Salinger

Do or Die by Leon Bing

There Are No Children Here by Alex Kotlowitz

My Posse Don't Do Homework by LouAnn Johnson

Fist, Stick, Knife, Gun by Geoffrey Canada

Warriors Don't Cry by Melba Patillo Beals

Classic Movies:

"Boyz In The Hood"

"The Breakfast Club"

"My Bodyguard"

"The Boy With Green Hair"

"Dead Poets Society"

"Mask"

"The Man Without a Face"

"Ordinary People"

"Charlie Bartlett"

"The Bronx Tale" "The Outsiders"

"The Sisterhood of the Traveling Pants"

Resources:

National School Safety Center Gangs In Schools:
  Breaking Up is Hard to Do www.schoolsafety.us

Wikipedia has information on Gang Clearance Task Forces

National Association of Adult Survivors of Child Abuse

http://naasca.org —look for section on grooming

Grooming for abusive relationships
  www.abuseandrelationshipsl.org

Grooming www.outofthefog.website

CHAPTER 6
SCHOOL, WORK AND RECREATION

"So this is college. I didn't miss a thing."
— **Marlon Brando in "The Freshman"**

School is often where young people are tested the most, if the pun is not too much. Here is where the teen learns to interact with other peers and with adults in authority. This is where he/she is tested against others in academics, sports, popularity and dexterity, where, as the saying goes, the rubber meets the road. It is where, sometimes more than in earlier school experiences, a young person is expected to interact with others in a cooperative fashion, often in groups, and hopefully to fit in.

Confucius is quoted as saying, "By three methods we may learn wisdom: First, by reflection, which is noblest; second, by imitation, which is easiest; and third, by experience, which is the bitterest." As much as we would like to tell our children about our own experience, so that they won't repeat our mistakes, we often find that children are generally not good historians. Since they don't generally want to learn of the mistakes of the past, they are doomed to repeat them. Thus the battles of the generations—we as parents want to protect our kids by preventing foreseeable mistakes, and their drive is to learn for themselves. At the same time, we are at the developmental stage where we are trying to simplify our lives, while they are at the developmental stage where they need to complicate theirs for the excitement of it.

Besides the natural developmental differences that occur at these different generations, there are other impediments to learning that some youth experience. We will talk about some of the mental illnesses and the impact of drugs and alcohol in later chapters, but there are other medical problems that can impact severely on learning and work relationships. We will talk about these, but first we will talk about attitudes that can get in the way.

Attitudes: We are verbal animals. All one has to do is to look around the room at an object and a name pops into mind. We have verbal symbols that we immediately attach to all objects. If it doesn't have a name, we make one up (that red thing, that big thing, etc.). People learn to think in words, and the words that we learn to use to think about ourselves, tend to color our perceptions of ourselves. Kids learn to think of themselves in certain ways from their environment. If they have been discouraged in doing things or in learning things, they may use words like "dumb" or "clumsy" or "slow" to describe themselves, and then learn to think of themselves in those terms. They may develop low self-esteem, low motivation to try certain things. They may become passive, or they may become angry and frustrated. Some overachieve beyond their abilities, expanding themselves. The school experience is very important for these reasons. It is where kids learn who they are, and the teen years are often critical for this, because it is precisely at this time that abstract thinking and reasoning come into the fore. It is when notions like justice, freedom, peace, fairness, beauty, evil, and many more such ideas become more predominant in the everyday thinking of these young people. It is also a time when limits and boundaries have to be placed, with adroitness and kindness, but firmness. It was Pascal who said, "It is not good to be too free. It is not good to have everything one wants." Also, to paraphrase G.B. Shaw, "There are two tragedies in a person's life. One is that he does not achieve the object of his dreams. The other is that he does." Thus, the most difficult job of parenting continues; the drift back and forth of being a friend to your kids and being intimate with them, listening carefully and giving them a kind ear at one moment, and having to step out of that role in the next to be a manager or an umpire, calling the shots and making decisions when the child shows that he is not yet ready to make this one appropriately. Kids will say they hate it, but if the structure is not there, they will panic and push the limits until you set them. This includes giving them a certain leeway at school, but only as long as they continue to do their jobs there, and if it becomes clear that they are not, stepping in and tracking them until they do.

Academics: The first and foremost reason that schools were brought into being was to teach information, whether it had to do with skills or with pure knowledge. Academics are an important ingredient in today's schools, though not the only ingredient. Remember, the main job of parenting is that of teacher, and schools are "in loco parentis" or, in other words, in place of the parents. The job of the schools is to teach, not just academics, but also values, survival in the world, getting along with others, and work skills. Yet, in order to survive in today's world, one must have a certain knowledge base. The old adage about history, for example, is true. "Those who do not pay attention to history are bound to repeat it."

Aristotle believed in the well-educated man. In his school, he taught metaphysics, natural science, rhetoric (politics) and poetics—everything from the very abstract philosophical thought, to the world around us, to the practical nature of persuasion, to the beauty of words and music and art. The explosion of knowledge and art in the Renaissance era was another stimulus to learning. Again, the emphasis was on the complete person, one who was well-rounded in the arts and the sciences and who was also skilled in the physical arts. Cyrano de Bergerac was the romantic era's idealization of such a Renaissance man. Our own era has developed an explosive technology and base of knowledge probably unmatched in any other era, mainly because we have developed the technology to increase its ability to explode exponentially by the very nature of its technology. We have to be careful not to get lost in the expanse of information and in the process of getting more and more of it, but to also be able to appreciate what we have already. In our computerized world, it is very easy to get caught up in our ability to rapidly get information, so that we work harder and harder to get it faster and faster, and then forget why we were looking for it. In order not to leave behind us the ability to make friends, develop intimacy, be able to appreciate beauty, develop speaking and listening skills, and problem solve with other people, it is important to keep in our school curricula things other than "the basics". Yet, we need to teach our children the academic skills needed to go on to be educated in a way that allows for competition in today's world.

Extracurriculars: History, Math, Science, Languages, Reading, Writing, Spelling; all are critical to education, but not all young people excel in these academic areas. It is important for youth to experience success in order to experience the desire to excel. Not all of us become college professors. Some of us need to become good plumbers, mechanics, musicians, artists, ball players, coaches, and dentists. We need to develop hobbies that carry us into our middle and old age without withering when our jobs are done. We need to have interests that keep our kids out of trouble with drugs and other illegal activities. The kid who is a good basketball player may find a way to go to college. The kid who is a bit nerdy may find his interest in chess or computers helps him to socialize with others who seek his knowledge or information. The kid who goes out for acting may develop a sense of confidence that he did not have before. Likewise for the kid with an artistic bent or the kid who begins to like the instrument he plays. It is important for kids to develop some sense of confidence in something that they do, whether it is social such as being a good dancer, physical such as being a good football player, or academic by having a knack for foreign languages or being a good mathematician.

Medical Problems: Besides attitudinal problems, there are some young people who have definitive medical problems. Some of these include: attention deficit disorder (ADD or ADHD), seizure disorders and learning disabilities. I would like to take some time to talk about all three here.

Seizures: There are many kinds of seizures. Essentially what a seizure is, is an electrical storm in the brain. When brain cells normally fire, they do so in synch with other cells, sending messages back and forth between different parts of the brain by depolarizing the membrane of the cell (meaning changing the electrical charge on the surface of the cell). This depolarization causes the release of minute quantities of chemical substance into the space between the cells. The receiving end of the next cell is sensitive to this substance which we will call a neurotransmitter substance. When it is stimulated in this way, the second cell passes on the message by depolarizing itself and thus "firing" or releasing its own neurotransmitter. With seizures, the problem arises when the cell membranes are especially sensitive and fire prematurely, sometimes all at once—thus we get an electrical storm, and all the other body cells which are to respond to the brain cells also do so. In a major seizure, the person may then lose consciousness, fall down and thrash his body about in violent movements. There are, however, lesser degrees of seizure.

The old classification of seizures was simple—grand mal (the one described above), petit mal (a brief period of lapse of consciousness, but not causing falling—rather causing a short period of staring and unawareness of surroundings, followed [as in all seizures] by a period of confusion), and psychomotor seizures (where the individual is not consciously aware of what is going on, but continues to partake in activities, usually a stereotyped kind of repetitive behavior peculiar to that person's seizure pattern, followed by the period of confusion on awakening). Now some seizures are called "absence" (a blank space of unawareness); others are called amyotonic (abrupt falling without necessarily having the thrashing movements—but which can be dangerous to the individual because of the problems with head injuries). There are seizures that can be triggered by certain tones of music, by reading certain words, by touching certain parts of the body, by a certain frequency of flashing lights. Interestingly, many of these latter types of seizure can be altered by methods of biofeedback as well as medication.

The thing to remember about seizures is that they are mostly treatable, but if gone unrecognized and untreated, they will interfere significantly with learning and could get worse. Imagine, if you would, the young person who is sitting in class listening intently to the teacher explain a lesson. As the instruction progresses, there is a sudden loss of awareness of what the teacher has been talking about for the last 30-40 seconds. The middle has gone out of the explanation. Most young people are too embarrassed to ask what they have missed and in addition the "post-ictal" confusion makes it more muddled, so the kid does his best and muddles on, often messing up the directions and the lesson. Such interruptions in the learning process can be confusing to the individual suffering them, and not always clearly in their awareness.

There are many types of medication that are very effective in preventing and treating seizures. Keep in mind that this is frequently a very treatable condition, and the physician experts most suited to treatment of these populations are neurologists, especially the more complicated or difficult cases.

Attention Deficit Disorder: This is a problem of attention or distractibility, though many times it is accompanied by hyperactive behavior. It could be included in the chapter on mental health problems, because it is also a significant cause of other kinds of distress in the individual as well as families, and often results in feelings or behaviors that leads to psychological distress, but I choose to talk about it here, because it tends to impact so much on school performance as well as peer relationships and self-esteem.

Hyperactivity is a general term and can be caused by a number of things including anxiety, drugs, head injuries, thyroid disease and other afflictions in addition to attention deficit disorder. The hallmark of this disorder is not hyperactivity, but problems with attention span. It may occur with or without hyperactivity and impulsivity. A person with this disorder may come to it in one of many ways. Sometimes it runs in families. Sometimes it is the result to some insult to the central nervous system which interferes with an important function of the brain, that is, to filter out all the extraneous stimuli that bombard it. The world outside to a person with ADD is like the earth getting bombarded by cosmic rays from space. Most of the time the atmosphere filters them out so that they are harmless, but if that filter were not there, the irradiation would be too much for us. The brain, too, filters out a lot of information that bombards us daily. We soon learn to "tune out" the things that would tend to distract us, allowing us to be able to focus on one thing at a time. Not so for the person with ADD. Every little thing going on around them is a distraction (someone walking by with a music box, a siren down the street, a plane going overhead, a dog barking, someone dropping a pencil), and this makes it very difficult for a person with ADD to focus for any length of time on one thing or to stay on track with school or work. Some people work very hard to compensate for this difficulty, but it takes a lot of energy. Some people learn to structure their lives around their ADD, but sometimes that isn't enough.

Signs: There are three major features of ADD, not all of which need be present: inattention, hyperactivity and impulsivity. Signs of inattention are:

1) Often not giving close attention to details or making careless mistakes in schoolwork, work, or other activities.

2) Often having difficulty sustaining attention in tasks or play activities.

3) Often not seeming to listen when spoken to directly.

4) Often not following through on instruction and failing to finish schoolwork, chores, or duties (not due to oppositional behavior but by failing to understand directions or "forgetting").

5) Often having difficulty organizing tasks and activities.

6) Often avoiding, disliking, or being reluctant to engage in tasks that require sustained mental effort (such as school work or homework).

7) Often losing things necessary for tasks or activities, such as toys, assignments, books, or tools.

8) Is often easily distracted by extraneous stimuli.

9) Is often forgetful in daily activities.

Signs of hyperactivity are:

1) Often fidgeting with hands or feet or squirms in seat.

2) Often leaving seat in classroom or in other situations in which remaining seated is expected.

3) Often running about or climbing excessively in situations in which it is inappropriate.

4) Often having difficulty playing or engaging in leisure activities quietly.

5) Often "on the go" or often acting as if "driven by a motor".

6) Often talking excessively.

Signs of impulsivity are:

1) Often blurting out answers before questions are completed.

2) Often having difficulty waiting one's turn.

3) Often interrupting or intruding on others, such as butting into conversations or games.

Treatment: We have learned over time that there are certain medicines of a stimulant nature that, for some reason, seem to be able to enhance the brain's ability to strain or filter out the massive amount of distractive stimuli that impinge on it during the time that these medicines are active in the body. They seem to boost the brain's ability to put up the filters and "tune out all the noise". Because they are of a stimulant nature, they are also capable of being abused by people who do not have ADD, and thus some of these medicines have gotten "bad press", though they do not appear to have addictive qualities for people who have ADD. Some of the commonly used medicines are: Ritalin, Dexedrine, and Adderal. In addition Clonidine, otherwise used for blood pressure, seems to sometimes be helpful. Several antidepressants such as Imipramine, Desipramine and Wellbutrin have also been used. In addition, another non-stimulant medicine called Strattera has been found to be effective in treating ADD/ADHD.

The best way to determine whether a person has ADD or not, is to have someone familiar with the disorder take a careful history. Sometimes questionnaires are helpful to get the kind of information needed. There is also a computerized test called the

TOVA (Test Of Variable Attention) that is helpful. After being diagnosed, it is important to discuss the problem and its treatment with someone familiar with the proper pharmacology to treat it. This is sometimes a pediatrician, more often a child psychiatrist. Untreated, this problem often leads the individual to view oneself as "dumb", annoying, or even bad. He may feel defeated, acting the class clown, because he sees that arena as one area in which he can at least be successful.

Alternative treatments include highly structured and individualized programs which sometimes work fairly well and sometimes not. Some people have used biofeedback techniques which use electroencephalogram leads to help people learn to alter their usual patterns of brain waves. This has been touted by some to be very effective, and indeed, I have spoken to both the treaters and the treated who say they have received great benefit from biofeedback, but long term studies are not yet available to say how effective they are.

Specific Learning Disabilities: In addition to Attention Deficit Disorder, there are numerous specific academic skills disorders that can interfere with learning. They include disorders of learning mathematics, writing and reading (dyslexia). There are also language and speech disorders, including disorders of articulation, of expressive language, and of receptive language. Most of these disorders involve difficulties in receiving concepts in the brain or of expressing concepts, some in the form of written words, some in the form of spoken words, or in the case of mathematics, in the form of non-verbal symbols. Typically, the people who are most expert at evaluating and treating such difficulties are those people trained in our schools in special education.

It should be kept in mind that these individuals with such disabilities are often intelligent people, but have a defect in their wiring, so to speak, and need to be taught other ways to compensate, or to find other ways to take in or express information. Such techniques are available to be taught.

Behavior Problems: This is a large but general category of referrals that come to us from schools. It includes a myriad of problems. They often include problems related to environment, but these may range from the depressed kid who shows it by acting angry, to the child with poor self-esteem who may have been sexually abused for months or years. It includes children who have had poor modeling by their peers or family, or who have just made poor choices and perhaps gotten away with some without getting caught and so have continued, thinking that they won't get caught. They include those kids whom we label as "conduct disordered" who get into trouble with truancy, the law, and with fighting, stealing, cheating and lying. They may also include those kids who are what we call "oppositional-defiant" who are over-responding to their adolescent needs for their autonomy and self-direction, and who do not want to follow the rules and directions that are imposed upon them by others in authority, including parents and teachers. Behavior problems are frequently merely signs of other problems that should be taken more seriously. Thus, the term behavior disorder is seen by me as a more generic term that points to some other issue that is going on for this kid. They are often learned behaviors and can therefore be relearned or unlearned.

Work: Work is often really started in the teen years as well. Though many children are taught how to do various chores and tasks for which they may get an allowance, many get their first jobs while teenagers. The training that helps them to do well in jobs often comes earlier, including money handling, cooperation, following directions, organization, taking responsibility, etc., but the out of home work experience measures and draws out the young person. It is where many young people first begin to get a sense of independence and of confidence in their own capabilities, how they relate to others different from their parental and sibling contacts and that of peers, and teachers, who are more like parental figures in many ways. Many young people, who work jobs, get a sense of direction from such activities that steers them in the path of furthering their education to be able to follow a particular career path, about which they might not have had a clue without the work experience. That career path might be in the direction of the activity of the job, or it may be a "wakeup call" that tells the kid that "no way do I want to work a job like this the rest of my life. I'm getting an education or some training to be able to do something else." Also, unlike school or parental directives, the relationship to a boss is a "real world" experience. At home, a child can say no; at school, a child can say no; the result is a confrontation, sometimes consequences, but never a dismissal from the family, and rarely a dismissal from school, unless for an egregious offense. At work, a no is simply followed by, "You're fired!" No further questions, no confrontation about fairness, just, "Get out of here!" and the young person knows this from the beginning, resulting in a totally different relationship from the beginning—much like the real world. Thus, often it is a good idea to encourage some forms of employment outside the home by your teen.

Problems At School And Work: One of the major problems that kids suffer from in both school and the work place is **poor self-esteem**. This may come about in a number of ways, but interferes with performance, because it interferes with what teens perceive of themselves being able to do with any success. As a result, they tend to try less hard, to stop their ambitions short of their true capabilities, and, all too often, to fall short of their original goals. Encouragement and planning successes are thus very important with young people who are struggling with self-esteem.

Low motivation can be caused by poor self-esteem, but this is not the only reason for it to occur. People can be in the habit of getting no credit for those things that are done well; they may feel there is little use in putting out 100% if there is not going to be any recognition when they do well. Drugs may be an issue in low motivation. The "low motivation syndrome" which is often referred to with marijuana use is an example. Difficulties with a particular subject may tend to decrease motivation in that class, as may a sense of frustration with a particular teacher.

Ironically, **overachieving** can sometimes be a problem at school or even at work. When a person pushes to the point that he is placed in a position of expectation by others in authority, sometimes he cannot keep up with the expectations and may fall short. Or, sometimes a child will overachieve to the point that he is placed with peers who have to work less hard to get the same results, with the consequence that he cannot easily keep up with his peers and finds himself falling behind, and getting discouraged.

Another area that gets a lot of kids in trouble is **acting out** behavior. The kid who gets a lot of attention in a negative way (maybe because he fails to do so in a positive way) is often one who is pinpointed as a troublemaker by his teachers and a clown by his peers, but the need tends to persist to continue to get attention in whatever way he can. The secret is to try to find a way that the kid can be successful without disrupting. Sometimes a kid can be steered, for example, in the direction of the drama department where he can channel his energies and exhibitionism in a positive direction. Another may be into the arena of sports, where he will also have to keep up his grades to stay eligible.

Passivity can be a significant problem. By passivity, we mean someone who sits back and lets things happen or not happen. Passivity in itself, is difficult, because others know that the kid has potential, but is not choosing to use it in a productive way, and most teens learn very quickly that they can outwait any adult, because time is on their side.

Passivity can be a powerful weapon in any teen's arsenal, while passive-aggressive behavior can be infuriating to an adult. By passive-aggressive we mean purposely doing things in a negative way to someone by being passive (e.g., allowing a sack of groceries to fall because of not wanting to carry it, but knowing that it contained a dozen eggs that would break; neglecting to lower the garage door, knowing that in that neighborhood, a brother's bike might well be stolen). Passivity can be very difficult to contend with, but sometimes it takes a return of similar behavior to turn it around. One ploy that I use for small children and teens alike is the no bank. This is a sheet of paper with the child's name on it. It is posted on the refrigerator or other accessible posting place. The rules are spelled out to the kid, as well as expectations. Nothing but his

118

name is on the paper, until he refuses a chore, neglects a rule, or takes more time to do it than is practical. Then a mark is put on the paper. With each refusal or "no", a mark is placed on the paper, signifying a "deposit" into his "no bank". Then when he wants something from you, you merely give him one of his "no's" back and erase one from the chart. If he gets angry and tears the chart down, it is very easy to put back up, only with the "poor memory" that parents tend to have, it is "very likely" that you will "forget" just how many were there in the first place and probably put a few more up than were there before. In addition, there will be at least one more because of breaking the rule of taking the chart down and destroying it. Another handy tool in dealing with passivity is the Sunday Box. This is a large trunk with a lock on it that can be stored in a handy place (like the garage). When things are left around that should be picked up or put away, and suggestions to do so are ignored, the items can be put in the Sunday Box and locked up until the following Sunday. It is especially handy for items of clothing, toys, walkmans, CD's, tablets, etc.

Money Misuse: Sometimes kids who have outside jobs tend to become so independent that they misuse their money, spending it on items that parents do not approve of, or acting as though parents should no longer have a say about what they do because they are self-sufficient (in terms of buying clothing, CD's, auto insurance, gasoline, etc. They often do not have a clue about all the expenses in running a household that are hidden (like the toothpaste, toilet paper, water bill, heat bill, laundry soap, telephone bill, grocery expenses—especially with a teenager, etc.). Sometimes a sitdown with the teen and going over the household expenses is useful. Sometimes an establishing of rules about what his money can be used for is helpful. If neither of those works, a system of monetary fines can be invoked; removal of the car keys regardless of whether he owns the car or not is legit, and one can always go to the Dept. of Motor Vehicles and have a minor child driver's license yanked if he is not cooperative. Auto insurance in most states has to be cosigned for by a parent for a minor child. It is important to let a child know that someone will be in charge of him, especially if that person is ultimately responsible for whatever behavior the child engages in under the law.

Recreation: Play is a very important item in every child's life from a very early age, and it doesn't stop with adolescence, nor with adulthood for that matter. In much of a child's life, play is built in as part of their schooling as well as part of their leisure time activities. It is just structured differently. The kind of play varies with age and sex, and it may be competitive or cooperative, but for a healthy child, it needs to be in place.

When children are younger, they tend to participate a lot in "parallel play", that is, they play with other children, but in a parallel fashion, alongside others but continuing in their own private pursuits. An example is the child who stacks blocks next to the child who is pushing a toy truck around. As they get older, they tend to interact more with one another. The truck may knock the block stack down, and a disagreement might ensue, but eventually they will probably get into a cooperative play that starts with building a stack of blocks and taking turns to knock it down. As I have mentioned elsewhere, adolescence is often seen as the "recapitulation" or repetition of earlier childhood experiences, but in a more global manner. Kids may find themselves participating in "parallel play" such as reading novels to themselves, while another builds a model, but they may also participate in cooperative ventures such as playing cards or chess. The cooperative play may be competitive, like sports (choosing sides to play football or basketball), chess, or competing in a poetry contest, or it may be less so like jamming in the garage with other kids in a makeshift rock band.

Competition tends to be very strong in teen activities, whether it be sports, drama, music, or academics. Even the kids who are playing cooperatively by jamming in the garage may have a competition in the big scheme of things that they are preparing for. They may be hoping to get better than the other band they heard, so they can get a paying gig in place of the others.

Whether we like it or not, play anticipates our kid's roles in the "real world", when they have reached maturity, and play is a very important aspect of their preparation for making it out there. Thus it is important to model good playing skills for our kids. As we learned before, the role of parent is essentially that of teacher. We must teach both intimacy and survival. It is therefore important to learn to mix it up with our kids in a playful way and not just model our serious side, so they can see that there is more to life than work and making money.

As our kids reach their teens, they will find themselves exposed to a lot of opportunities for play and recreation that can be dangerous. I can recall watching young men of 16-17 jumping off a bridge over a small river into the water about 40 feet below. The rock walls of the small canyon seemed ominous to me, but fortunately no one was hurt that day, yet every summer a young man or woman seems to have a neck injury in the emergency room where I have spent some time, because of some slip or accident in doing just some similar stunt. There are many dangers out there, and unfortunately teens tend to not see themselves as vulnerable, so it is important to lay down the law as parents about what kinds of recreational activities are allowed, not that it will always be of use to have such a meager bit of reassurance, but at least we know we did our best to keep the risks down.

Much of play and recreation in adolescence takes the form of competitive team sports, yet there are many youth who are not adept enough at sport to make the teams. Thus it is important to help your kids find those recreational outlets that best suit their strengths. By doing so, it allows them to build their self-esteem and their identity, and gives them the confidence they need to go on and tackle other difficult things in their lives.

Bullying: With the number of homicidal attacks in schools in the last 15 years or more, it is important to address the aspect of bullying. It has become known that bullying is an important factor in the genesis of at least some of these attacks. Bullying can be verbal, physical or cyber. It can be done individually or collectively in a group. Kids who feel isolated from their peers, alienated and estranged and "on the outside" of their peer groups will sometimes find themselves looking for "how to get even" or somewhere and somehow to express their rage, and sometimes a means to get recognition. Many schools have become aware of the need to have a "zero tolerance" for expressions of violence, and have put into place programs to minimize cliques and labels. It is of great importance as parents to voice your concerns about these issues and to make sure that your schools are on top of them. Be involved. Be on top of any issue that may surface having to do with mistreatment of any child by their peers. Do not be afraid to address these issues with the school administration if they arise. Remember, it may not be your kid today, but it could be tomorrow.

In this chapter, we have tried to look at places where teens spend a good portion of their lives, and at the importance of looking beyond grades and the concrete details of what material the kids are getting crammed into their heads and the importance of developing self-esteem and confidence.

Pearls For Parents:

1) There is a lot of luck in how kids fall into success, like the teachers they happen to get, the friends they meet, etc. There is something to say for <u>planning a success</u>. Help make it happen. Look at what kinds of things they happen to be good at, and structure some opportunities. It may not always work out, but eventually some things may fall into place. However, be careful not to make it look like you have maneuvered it too much, or the tendency is for the teen to go in the opposite direction.

2) If your child has something suspicious going on, pursue it. If you suspect a medical problem or a learning disability, pursue it. There is often a "we—they" attitude that can develop between teachers and parents. Don't let the notion that you may be seen as a "pushy parent" stop you. If you don't stand up for your kid and try to get services, who will? He/she may otherwise go unnoticed as having something wrong until too late to effectively intervene, and in spite of all the good intentions, an opportunity will be lost.

Resources:

Internet:

Google CHADD (Children & Adults with ADD)

Wikipedia for information about bullying
  – also www.stopbullying.gov

Also – www.dare.org/bullying and www.verywell.com

Books:

Driven to Distraction by Hallowel and Ratey

Crisis in the Classroom by Jonathon Kozol

Reviving Ophelia by Mary Pipher

Classic Movies:

"The Flamingo Kid"

"A Bronx Tale"

"My Bodyguard"

"Rocket Science"

"An Education"

Chapter 7
SEX AND INTIMACY

"Each lover has some theory of his own
About the difference between the ache
Of being with his love, and being alone:"
— W.H. Auden "Are You There"

When we speak of sex and intimacy, we often interchange the terms, yet intimacy can and does occur without sex, and sex certainly does sometimes occur without intimacy. Intimacy is best defined as being in a close, familiar, and affectionate or loving personal relationship with another person or group. Sex usually refers to the act of sexual intercourse, or to the behavior that leads in that direction.

If we examine sexual behavior in adolescents, we must look again at the notions arrived at in the chapters on communication and development. We must remember that **"normal" can be viewed in at least four different ways—statistical, healthy, utopian, and process**. We must also remember that what may be "totally embarrassing" or disgusting to a 13 yr. old, would be a great joke to a 17 yr. old. In other words, the range of sexual behavior in teens is very wide, depending partly on the level of development.

How we view sexual behavior in terms of normality depends on the perspective one takes. If we look at what is **statistically normal**, we find that many young people these days participate in sexual behavior. Some blame this on the "sexual revolution" and the loosening of mores that started in the sixties. Some blame a deterioration in "family values". There are complex reasons for the changes in sexual behavior of teens, not the least of which may include the fact that people tend to be much more open about talking about it. The issue is, however, whether it is "normal" in other ways than statistically. Is it healthy? Is it ideal? How has the process of sexual maturation changed with changes in our society?

I would purport that sexual behavior among adolescents, for the most part, is not necessarily normal in terms of being **healthy**. Sure, a young healthy boy or girl is going to have physical drives, and that is healthy. These young people will also be attracted to each other and even fall in love, and that is healthy. The problem is that most young people who are having sexual relations tend to mix up the sex part with the intimacy part. The nature of young love is that it is often short-lived, and when sex enters the picture, it is much more difficult to extricate oneself from a now unwanted relationship, than it would be if sex had not entered the picture. All too often, what masquerades as love is often a combination of hormones and lust, as well as perhaps genuinely liking the person. All too often, people get very emotionally hurt in the process and find it difficult to trust in subsequent romantic relationships.

Then, too, there is the ever-present issue of **sexually transmitted diseases**. AIDS or HIV had become epidemic in this country to the point that we had almost forgotten about Herpes, and the old standbys like syphilis, gonorrhea and Chlamydia have not taken a hike. We also have to be especially aware of Human Papillomaviruses, which are difficult to detect, but can cause significant cancers as kids get older.

When the birth control pills became the way to go, barriers to disease (condoms) sometimes went by the wayside. I always remember making rounds on a cancer ward with a resident while a medical student. He pointed out a patient and said, "You wouldn't think that a sweet little old lady like that would have cancer, would you, but she does." Later, I thought of that in the V.D. clinic. "You wouldn't think a beautiful clean-looking girl like that would have the clap, would you?" But she did.

Then there is the issue of what to do in case of **pregnancy**. Abortion? The mother has to live with that the rest of her life.

Some do it better than others. Give it up for adoption? Easier said than done. People remain haunted by this decision, both kids and parents. Look at the industry that has burgeoned around searching for biological parents and for children given up years ago. Keep the baby? Who takes care of it? The mother? The grandparents? What does the mother have to give up to become a single parent? How does she support the child? Do they live in poverty? If she marries the father, are either of them ready for a life together?

Thus, my attitude is that sexual activity, in and of itself, is good, but it is not a great idea for the wrong reasons or at the wrong time, no matter how much people feel that they are in love. It is far from normal in terms of the **ideal**, and though young people may be **developmentally** ready, in terms of their developmental process from a physical standpoint, our society today makes it very difficult for people to start having families in their teens, without completing their education or some form of training to be able to be employable, and as I alluded to above, emotional development must also be considered.

There are definitely **male-female differences** that we should take into consideration, as well as the fact that age and experience make a significant impact on these differences. First of all, in the early years of adolescence, girls tend to mature emotionally much more quickly than boys. This is not true across the board, but generally girls tend to be much more facile with words and in carrying on a conversation than boys the same age, and they often tend to become more interested in boy-girl relationships, while boys are struggling with other means of grappling with their emerging identities. As the boys get older, they get better at it, but girls often tend to be spending time with boys a year or two older. Herein lies another problem. Boys, as they get older, tend to become more interested in pursuing a more active sex life, and can become more aggressive in seeking out sexual partners. Again, this is not true across the board, but as they get older, both sexes tend to become less inhibited about overt sexual word play, and thus sometimes subsequently less inhibited about sexual behavior altogether.

Boys tend to be initially attracted to girls because of their looks. Girls also like guys who are good-looking, but they also tend to be attracted to personality more so than boys do, at least initially. The old saying goes that boys tend to fall in love with a girl's looks, while girls tend to fall in love with a boy's mind. It is probably an exaggeration, but there is some truth in that sentiment.

Masturbation (solitary sex): Some people consider masturbation sinful. At one time excessive sexual energy was blamed for just about every non-contagious disease in history. There was a time when boys were trussed up at night to go to bed in what amounted to straight jackets, so they wouldn't "play with themselves" at night and sap their bodies of valuable sexual energy. Insanity was sometimes blamed on masturbation, as were "weak eyes". The joke goes that the father was warning the young adolescent not to masturbate, because if he did it too much, he would go blind, and the boy meekly asked his father if he could do it to the point that he just needed to wear glasses. Such a story emphasizes the extent of sexual urge in young boys. Girls too have sexual urges and also masturbate, though perhaps not to the degree that boys do. For women, sex often tends to be more a whole body phenomenon. It involves touch in many parts of her body. For men, it can be that as well, but especially in the teen years, tends to reside mostly in the penis. Like one woman said, " a man's sexuality is like Florida. It just hangs out there."

Boys, as they awaken to their sexuality, tend to have many embarrassing moments such as when they unexpectedly develop an erection in a classroom, practically involuntarily, and then may have to stand to recite. They tend to be so aware of their erection that they feel the whole world is staring at the corncob that is extruding from the front of their pants. Such a sudden onset of tumescence can occur as well in the shower as they wash, in bed as the friction of the sheets rubs their penis, or as they are just sitting on the toilet. "Wet dreams" are not uncommon in adolescent boys (usually accompanied by an erotic dream in which ejaculation occurs). Boys often awaken embarrassed to find their bed wet and sticky, and not knowing how to dispose of the "evidence". Boys soon find that they can experience the same pleasures that occur in their wet dreams by masturbating. It starts simply enough, and sometimes occurs up to 3-4 times per day. Usually boys use visual stimuli to come to climax. Thus they enter their sexual fantasy seeing women primarily as sexual objects, because if they began to think of them as friends in their sexual fantasies, they might begin to lose the goal they are trying to achieve at the moment, which is to reach orgasm. Unfortunately, at this age, thinking tends to be rather black and white or either/or. A girl is either seen as sweet and pure or as someone he would not want to bring home to mama. At the moment he is masturbating, he is not interested in a relationship, but to get off. The problem is that as the habit of visualizing women in this way emerges, it is more difficult to develop relationships with women that are not tainted with self-directed sexual satisfaction. Some don't learn very well how to make friendships first, allowing respect to emerge, and develop sexual relationships later. Some find that when they marry the girl of their dreams eventually, she is just as interested in sex as he is, and that may tend to be confusing after spending so much time viewing girls as a contrast between madonna and prostitute.

Masturbation is not a male only phenomonon. Girls also experiment with sexual touching, and some learn to reach orgasm this way. Since the 1960's the social pressure on girls has lifted in regard to sexual interests and more open sexual behavior. There is more social permission to be interested in sex. For a woman, sex is still a total body experience, but Freud was wrong. Women are not restricted to vaginal orgasms. They can and do have orgasms with clitoral stimulation, and girls do enjoy sex.

Masturbation is a very common phenomenon. Is it normal? Let's go back to our model. **Statistically it is extremely normal. It can be healthy or unhealthy, depending on circumstances. It is not ideal** sex, but then it is not ideal for teens to be actively participating in sex indiscriminately, and teens are not ready for committed long-term relationships, so it is more ideal for teens to practice their sexual behavior without partners until their social skills and emotional growth has been readied for more mature and lasting relationships. **In terms of process**, it is a means of growing into one's sexuality and learning about one's body in preparation for a more active and healthy sex life.

Non-intimacy motivations for sex: Although intimacy would seem to be a major reason for having sex, and can be a strong factor, there are a number of reasons other than intimacy that drive people to sexual behavior. We will talk about some of them now.

Anger is clearly one reason why some sexual activity takes place. The girl or boy who is angry with the person who has just broken up with him/her may result in that person looking for the next available or vulnerable person to either take the anger out on or to show the other ex that he/she is not unwanted by someone else. Having sex with someone else may be a very clear way to be hurtful to the ex-partner, or it may be a way to direct anger to another person of the same sex.

Power can be clearly sought through sex. It may be a way to control someone else or to show who is in charge. By threatening sex with others, by withholding intimacy, by flirting with others, all can be used to control, which is the hallmark of power.

Acting out often shows up in sexual behavior. It is again a way to exert one's will, for example, by showing parents that the child will do what one wants inspite of directions to do the opposite.

We cannot ignore the influence of **peer pressure**. Undoubtedly, the influence of peers can be strong, particularly with kids who are not strongly aware of their own personhood, but who tend to be influenced by others and are not secure in their own identities.

Prostitution does occur with teens. Sometimes it is a matter of survival, especially in a situation where a kid is living on the streets. Sometimes it is the aftermath of a rape or sexual molesting situation, where a kid has poor self-esteem as a result of that trauma, and thinks no better of himself/herself than to continue with the same degrading behavior. Sometimes it is just for the money, or for the power, or the anger.

The fact that a kid is involved in sexual behavior, as one can see, is not always just because the kid is infatuated or dragged by hormones into "the dance without steps". Sometimes the motivations are very complex, and they may require someone other than the parents talking to the kid, since most kids have some things, especially on the topic of sex, that they just don't want to talk to their parents about.

Sexual assault, sexual harrassment and sexual abuse: Sexual assault is, unfortunately, in our day and time, a reality to be guarded against and one to take precautions against. Unfortunately, many young people are so invigorated by their good health and energy, that they feel invincible and feel that they can handle themselves in almost any situation. As a result, sometimes good judgment is put aside and young people put themselves into situations that can be risky or even dangerous. Unfortunately as well, we find in our schools and at extracurricular activities, a tendency by some to intimidate others and take liberties in a sexual way that amounts to harassment. Some of our kids are exposed as well to sexual abuse. This occurs primarily to girls, but is not limited to them. Thus it is important to help our kids to find ways of dealing with this kind of behavior.

One of the biggest problems in combating unwanted sexual behavior is the **grooming** behavior on the part of the perpetrator. In the case of sexual abuse, the perpetrator often advances slowly, but with the definite goal in mind to gradually weaken resistance to his advances by insisting on the fact that there is a friendship here and that the intention is not to be hurtful. At the same time, the perpetrator may act hurt if there is any insinuation that anything else is the case. As the behavior becomes more sexual, the attitude often changes to one of blame. It is the victim's fault for leading him on. If she tells, he will let everyone know how she enticed him into this behavior, and so on. The implication is that everyone will know about her sexual promiscuity, her parents will be hurt, her friends will abandon her, and on and on. The child often feels trapped and continues in the unwanted behavior as it escalates and things get worse.

Children need to be taught from a very early age (since there are predatory people out there) that any behavior that feels uncomfortable or unwanted should be reported to someone who is seen as safe (usually the parents) so that those safe people can help to sort it out with the child. It is very important not to dismiss too quickly as improbable, any reporting of unusual or inappropriate behavior that a child brings to us. It should be listened to and checked out in the context of that child's history and previous behavior and track record. This should be the case with young children as well as our teens, and the child should be encouraged to report any unwanted behavior or anything that does not feel right, including behavior of peers at school or other activities.

One of the most common forms of sexual assault is **date rape**. It is often unreported because the girl is led to believe that she is partly responsible, that she led him on, that she really wanted to participate. Because she knows the boy, and because she may like him, and probably was taking pleasure in some of the preliminary "necking" that likely took place, the girl is frequently convinced that this is so.

Ruffies: Use of Ruphinol (Rohypnol or flunitrazepam) by some unscrupulous individuals, is a way to drug an unsuspecting victim into a state of intoxication which also leaves the individual with little memory of what has happened to her. Often it is slipped into a drink, leaving the victim dizzy, dazed, unable to effectively resist a sexual assault and often having little memory of what happened over an extended period of time. Education about this kind of assault is very important to young adolescents.

The sequellae of unwanted sexual advances and involvement often include feelings of low self-esteem, guilt, depressed mood, self-denigrating behavior, and sometimes even behavior that is self-harming. Unfortunately, if the child accepts responsibility (other than that of using poor judgment—which is not uncommon in teens) for either sexual assault or abuse, or even harassment, there is often a change in demeanor, in mood, and in behavior. Girls sometimes feel that as long as they have been "promiscuous", they may as well live up to their new-found status in life, and it is often a way they find to continue to be angry at themselves and to punish themselves by putting themselves even further into behavior that they don't like in themselves.

As parents, if we see a sudden change in personality or mood, it is important to check out what is going on. Ruling out drugs, it may well be that there has been some significant event that has occurred, and talking it over may help. Acceptance of anything that happened, whether the result of poor judgment or not, will go a long way to healing. Also, it would often help to get the child professional help with someone who has dealt with situations like this in the past.

Sexually Transmitted Diseases: This is an area where a little knowledge may be a very useful thing. Looking at historical literature from early times tells us that infectious diseases have often accompanied "promiscuous" sexual behavior. The bible offers us several such references. Hippocrates is said to have been the first to describe gonorrhea in early Greece. There is evidence of surgical and medical treatment of venereal diseases in early Egyptian papyri. Avicenna of Baghdad (980-1037) and Moses Maimonides of Cordoba (1135-1204) both wrote about urethral discharges in the middle ages. There was a syphilis outbreak in the 15th century and the English called it the Spanish pox, while the Spanish called it the French pox, etc. Some think syphilis came back to Spain from the new world, and there is some evidence that it did exist among the natives of America before explorers came to these parts, or it may have been the other way around.

Sexually transmitted diseases have been with us a long time, but there are many types. I will try to differentiate the commoner varieties. However, before doing that, I would like to point out **some critical information that can be life-saving**. This has to do with **Human Papillomaviruses**. HPV falls into 2 categories – 1) low risk viruses that cause skin warts that occur around the genitalia, anus, mouth and throat. They can also cause recurrent respiratory papillomatosis, or growths in air passages that lead from the mouth and throat to the lungs; 2) high risk HPV's which can cause cancers.

HPV's are the most common sexually transmitted infections in the United States. The Centers for Disease Control and Prevention estimate that more than 90% of men and 80% of women will be infected with some form of HPV at some time in their lives. Around half of these will be the high risk type. Most high risk HPV infections occur without any symptoms, go away within 1-2 years, and do not cause cancer. Some HPV infections, however, can persist for many years (without symptoms) and can lead to cell changes that, untreated, can lead to cancers – cervical, anal, oropharyngeal (mouth & throat, tonsils, soft palate, tongue), and sometimes rarer cancers such as vulvar or penis.

Transmission of HPV's: Anyone who has been engaged in skin to skin sexual contact, including vaginal, anal, or oral sex can get HPV. As with any sexually transmitted disease, it is more likely to occur when one of the partners has had sex with many other partners, but a person who has only had one partner can get HPV.

Prevention: The Food and Drug Administration has approved 3 vaccines to prevent HPV infections, but they are not effective in treating established infections. Condoms will not likely provide consistent nor reliable protection against infections. There is currently no treatment for infections that are not associated with cell changes, e.g. warts, respiratory tumors, precancerous changes in the cervix and cancers can be treated.

<u>**The most recommended method to prevent the occurrence of cancer as the person gets older is to make sure the pre-teen at age 11-12 receives the immunization for HPV. It is important that the complete series be received, otherwise there is only partial immunization.**</u>

Bacterial Infections: Gonorrhea (Neisseria gonorrheae—common name is **clap**)—results in a pustular urethral or rectal discharge in males, similar discharge in women as well as vaginal, but also in severe internal infection in females (pelvic inflammatory disease) often resulting in sterility from the scarring in the fallopian tubes which allow the transport of eggs from the ovaries to the uterus, or in ectopic (tubal) pregnancies. Sterility can also occur in men. **There may be no symptoms, especially in women.** It can also disseminate to other parts of the body to cause infections there, such as in the joints. It is acquired from direct contact with infected mucous membranes of the genitals, mouth, or rectum. Penicillin has historically been the treatment of choice, but there are now strains that are penicillin-resistant. First symptoms occur in 2-30 days.

Syphilis: (treponema pallidum—common names are **syph, bad blood, lues**)—there are three stages in this disease. The first is the local site of infection called a "hard chancre" and is a usually non-tender ulcer at the site of inoculation, often on the penis or the vagina. It appears 10 to 90 days after being infected and eventually disappears. Within a few weeks to months, a secondary stage begins with a systemic illness, characterized by low-grade fever, malaise, sore throat, headache, swollen lymph nodes, and a skin rash, often including the soles of the feet and the palms of the hands. This tends to subside, but the syphilis goes underground, so to speak. The third stage of syphilis is the most destructive. It can result over years in cardiovascular problems, such as widening of the aorta and resulting heart failure. Neurosyphilis, which affects the brain and spinal cord, causes loss of sense of position, paralysis and dementia is another late stage result. Penicillin has historically been the treatment of choice, but again, there may be some syphilis that can be resistant to penicillin. First symptoms occur in 10-90 days, and transmission is by direct contact with the infected area.

Chancroid: (Hemophilus ducreyi)—an ulcerative disease that often affects the external genitalia. Unlike the "hard chancre" of syphilis, this "soft chancre" is often very tender, especially in males. The incubation period is usually 4-7 days and the presenting problem is usually related to the ulcer or tenderness in the surrounding lymph glands. Tetracycline was historically the treatment of choice; again, there can be resistant strains.

Chlamydia: (chlamydia trachomatis)—In industrial western society virtually all chlamydial infections are transmitted sexually. Unlike other bacteria, chlamydia lives within other cells of the body, destroying them, not in the extracellular space. It can cause Lymphogranuloma venereum, an ulcerating condition which erodes the skin of the genital area, but it can also cause non-symptomatic infection, especially in males. Sometimes it will cause urethritis (seepage of pus from the penis), but in females it is much more destructive, and can cause much the same damage that gonorrhea does, including sterility. It is probably the most common STD treated in the U.S. these days. Again, this STD is caused by direct contact with infected mucous membranes. Usual onset is in 7-21 days.

Donovanosis: (Calymmatobacterium gramulomatis)—pretty rare in western countries, but not so rare in developing countries. Results in genital or anal non-tender but disfiguring ulcerative-looking lesions.

All of the bacterial diseases above are susceptible to antibiotic treatment, but some have developed resistant strains to the usual antibiotics, resulting in the need to go to newer and sometimes more expensive drugs to which the organism has not yet developed an immunity, if they can be found or are available.

Viral: HIV/AIDS (human immunodeficiency virus)—I cannot stress the importance of this disease enough. Again, most teens tend not to think of themselves as vulnerable, but this virus has been epidemic in some parts of the world, and still a disease to be very aware of in this country. It may surface after many months— up to 10 years. It is transmitted via body fluids, so that means saliva, seminal fluid, secretions in the female vagina and blood. It first becomes apparent after infection as a fever, sore throat, swollen glands, etc., resembling a cold. There may be weight loss, diarrhea, fatigue, tiredness, recurrent infections, sore throat, or skin blotches, or there may be no symptoms. It is **not a gay disease**. It is transmitted by heterosexual as well as homosexual contact, and by the indiscriminate use of infected needles where drug abuse occurs, or by receiving contaminated blood products (e.g. hemophiliacs who received blood transfusions prior to the testing of blood, once we became aware of the disease). The disease attacks the immune cells of the body, resulting in the growing lack of ability to fight off "opportunistic" infections, by other agents that would otherwise be easily fought off by a healthy immune system. People who die often succumb to such opportunistic diseases.

Genital Herpes: Caused by the same virus that causes "cold sores" and usually has its onset in 2-20 days. The virus tends to lie dormant under the skin until the immune system is weakened by fighting off another illness, or until the body is under some assault (e.g. surgery, sunburn, a cold). It then tends to flare up, causing painful ulceration that can take many days to subside. Genital herpes is transmitted by an individual who has an active lesion that comes in contact with mucous membrane and with the mild trauma of sexual activity. First episodes of genital herpes may be accompanied by systemic symptoms (fever, lassitude, headache, aching muscles) and may include multiple genital and extragenital sites, sometimes even in the central nervous system. Subsequent symptoms usually involve the genital sites, and are usually not as severe as the first episode. There is a possible link with disease and cervical cancer in women.

Hepatitis: The main means of transmission of this virus is by the oral-anal route. It can be aquired in sexual behavior, most often among homosexuals who may be having oral-anal contact. It can be transmitted to others by sexual contact, or by shared needles in drug using individuals. Some of the complications can be liver cancer, cirrhosis of the liver, chronic hepatitis, or even death. Usual onset is 60-90 days after contact.

Critters: We don't want to forget the little critters that can parasitize us, and that are frequently enough picked up as hitchhikers during sex.

Lice: The main louse that infests the genital region is the crab louse (Pthirius pubis). Under a microscope, it resembles a crab, thus the slang term "the crabs". It lays eggs on hairs and the adult depends on blood to live. It attaches to the skin, injects saliva with a clot-preventing substance and ingests blood. Also fondly referred to by those who have not had them as "crotch crickets" or "cooties".

Scabies: This is a form of mite (Sarcoptes scabiei—common name is "the seven year itch") that can be transmitted through sexual contact or by close physical contact. It moves rapidly over the human skin until it finds a spot to burrow under the skin where it lives for the next 30 days or more. It almost immediately begins to lay eggs under the skin to hatch and mature. These form adult mites in 10 days. In infected sexually active young adults, transmission is likely. The longer the contact, the more likely the transmission. Brief sexual contact is not as likely to transmit the pest as when two people spend the night together.

Protozoans: Trichomonas (trichomonas vaginalis—commonly called "trich") is a one-celled animal with a flagellum or tail. It results in a commonly sexually transmitted infection that usually shows up in 7-30 days. It causes an inflammatory response resulting in vaginal discharge in women and urethral discharge in men. It is most commonly treated with Flagyl (metronidazole).

Intestinal Protozoa: Sometimes intestinal parasites can be transmitted during sexual activity, especially by oral-anal contact. Such infections include: Giardia lamblia (giardiasis or "beaver fever"), Entamoeba histolytica (amoebiasis), and Cryptosporidium.

Fungi: Candida: (candida albicans)—This is the yeast infection that is most common in women, but in 20% of male partners of women with recurrent vaginal candida infections, colonization of yeast is found. It most commonly occurs in uncircumcised males. In women, it results in a vaginal infection with itching, burning, and a creamy vaginal discharge. It is often non-symptomatic in males.

Pregnancy: Let us look at another issue that has been with humankind since the beginning—unwanted pregnancy, or as one of my mentors called it on rounds, an "inadvertent primipara". Unfortunately for some, pregnancy can and does occur with the first "sexual indiscretion". Sometimes it just presents itself after a series of indiscriminate sexual behaviors. It can also occur as a result of rape. Regardless of how it occurs, one has several choices of action. The three main choices of any consequence are abortion, keeping the child, or giving it up for adoption, and there are many variations on how each of these may be done. I have seen young women find out about a pregnancy and try to kill themselves, or at least make some gesture in that direction. Rarely would that lead to a termination of the pregnancy. Usually it would result in some sympathy and problem solving, some counselling and planning. These same results can occur without the danger of an overdose or other such means of causing harm to oneself or to the fetus.

Sometimes the mother-to-be tries to avoid thinking about the pregnancy; however, using denial (not a river in Egypt) can only be successful for so long.

Abortion: Great controversy surrounds this choice. Some people are very explicit in seeing this as murder. Others see it as a woman's choice as to how to live their lives. Whatever the decision in regard to terminating or not terminating a pregnancy, it should not be one that is taken lightly. There are definitely some people who should not be raising children or exposing them to a very tawdry and cruel life, yet the decision to abort a fetus is often one that haunts people for many years, and can leave them with a yearning to have been able to reverse that decision. Certainly, if this option is to be considered, (and I understand that for some it is not considered to be an option) counseling should be sought so that all the ramifications can be looked at.

Adoption: This is a choice that has been seen by some in the past as a straight-forward solution to an unwanted pregnancy, yet it is not as simple a solution as one might imagine. A child may be very wanted by the accepting family, but the attachment that develops is not always the same as the attachment that a mother develops in carrying a child for nine months in her belly. Sometimes the attachment is easy and uneventful, but sometimes it is not so smooth. If a child is older at the time of adoption, the bonding or attachment is even more strained. Children aware of the adoption often struggle with feeling different from other family members, and especially as they reach adolescence, when issues of identity surface in any normal teenager, these same issues become paramount for the adopted child. Thus, if a pregnancy choice is for adoption, it is my opinion that some form of open adoption is best, that is, that the option for contact between the child and birth parent is left in such a way that such a connection can be made at some time in the future as would be deemed appropriate by all the parties of the "adoption triad".

Keeping the baby: This is another difficult choice. Many things need to be considered—how old is the mother? How mature is the mother? Is the mother self-sufficient? Is the mother going to be married? Is the father involved? Will he pay support? Will the grandparents be involved in raising the child? Are they willing or able to do so? Is there conflict between mother and grandparents? Is the mother marketable for a job? Does the mother need to complete her education? What about the father's education and marketability? Is marriage in the picture? Is it a good idea if it is? A myriad of questions, and these are just the beginning. Again, some good counselling to make sure that the choice in this direction is well-informed.

Unwanted Children: The history of the world shows us that we have not done well with our unwanted children. Novelists from Dickens to Alice Walker and Maya Angelou have shown us pain in children. Prevention is the best means of keeping unwanted children from showing up, and we need to not just assume that our kids are smart, good kids who know better, but

140

to also put enough structure in their lives to make it difficult for them to have the kind of "accident" that results in pregnancy, because good kids get pregnant too.

Teen marriages: In this day and age, teen marriages do not last as long statistically, as marriages among people who marry at a later age, say in their twenties. First of all, people who marry young are not yet fully developed emotionally. The person who gets married at 16 is often a totally different person at age 21. The 21 year old person has had a chance to mature, to develop notions and feelings that were not accessible at age 16. Likewise, the choices a person may make in choosing a partner might be totally different at a later age. What one likes to do at 16 may change completely by the time one is in his/her twenties (e.g. choices of music, of movies, of recreation, of humor, of appreciation of things, of places to relax, of what one enjoys reading, etc.). The problem is that people often begin to grow in different directions, and sometimes apart, through no fault of either partner.

The other thing that occurs in a "hurry up" marriage where a child is on the way, is that the couple has not had a chance to get to know each other without the presence of the child in the picture. They don't know each other very well without the influence on their relationship of the child. Sure, they knew each other for a "long time" before the birth of the baby, but they never really lived with one another to see how he forgets to pick up his socks, or she leaves her bras hanging in the bathroom, or how he leaves his dishes on the counter for her to take care of, or how she talks for hours on the phone to her friends. The list goes on. They didn't get to know each other as friends before they became lovers and then, precipitously, parents. It often results in a more difficult kind of "me-mine" relationship that emphasizes the loss of individuality of each partner rather than focusing on the blending of the individuals into a unit of family through friendship and appreciation of their differences.

All too often, when couples have been married awhile, and have never had the opportunity to date a lot or to meet other prospective partners that they checked out to get a sense of what it is in a mate that they were looking for, the time may come when their curiosity in others is aroused. They may want to experience someone other than this one partner that they have known. They may become disillusioned with this familiar person with whom they have spent so many years. They may feel bored. The recipe for difficulties in a marriage is there.

Peer pressure: Yes, it is there. Young people certainly respond differently to it. Part of this difference is based on temperament, part on history, part on choice. There are certainly those kids who are stubborn in their own right, and who make decisions about their sexuality and stick to those decisions, no matter how their peers are trying to influence them. There are others who tend to be easily swayed by others. There are kids who are wanting affection and closeness badly enough that they believe what they want to believe, namely, that the persons who are trying to persuade them to become sexually involved, are truly in love with them, and not just horny. (As adults, most of us know, for example, that a teen-age boy with an erection is likely to tell a girl in the back seat of a car just about anything in order to get into her pants, including, "I love you.") In fact, it may actually be true that love is felt, but the nature of relationships at this age is such that they are often short-lived, and what may feel like love today may fade to a fond or even bitter memory, and pregnancy and STD's are more than a fleeting memory.

Combating peer pressure starts early. Talking with young teens and preteens about their choices, their rights to their own bodies, their sense of honor and respect for themselves, their ability to be who they are without the need to have validation from their peers, and the nature of true friendship (friends care for what is best for you and not for themselves at your expense) will help your kids to be prepared to make better choices. However, in addition to talking to your kids, remember that it is important to keep your eyes open, set limits, keep your own eyes on your kids' boundaries, and be clear about your rules and expectations. If you loosen up on your kids' boundaries, it tends to model for the kids that it is OK to let down. They also may need to use parents as the "bad guys" that won't let them do some things, so it doesn't look like they are saying no, but doing so in order to live with these "unreasonable people who run my life". I personally would take pride in being depicted in this way, and it is a useful "out" for the kid.

Condoms: Whether or not to promote condom use among teens is a very controversial issue. I will be looking at the religious issues in another chapter, but it is important to look at the health issues in this chapter. To not address the use of condoms in this context would be tantamount to neglect.

Is promoting condom use the same as giving teens permission to have sex? Or is it a means of protecting them from disease and unwanted pregnancy? Are condoms really safe? Isn't abstinence better? Do they really protect people from disease?

There are certainly those who say that the use of condoms is not as safe as abstinence, but the problem is that a considerable amount of the teen population engages in sexual activity, and those who do, continue to be at risk. It is accurate to say that the use of condoms in those who do engage in sexual activity does significantly decrease the incidence of disease and unwanted pregnancy. There are those who say that pathologic agents such as viruses are smaller than the pores that are present in latex condoms. This may be true, but it is also true that viral agents like HIV are hitchhikers who travel on the backs of large and complex proteins that are present in bodily fluids and which are too large to pass through the pores of the latex. It is clear that condoms are not 100% effective, but the regular use in those who regularly engage in sex does decrease the odds against infection and pregnancy to a dramatic degree. In the population that is intending to continue to engage in sexual behavior, it is both smart and healthy, for the sake of our total population, to keep the incidence of disease down. With the prevalence of the HIV virus alone, it is neglectful to allow our teens to continue to practice unsafe sex without at least giving them the needed information that can help to protect them.

Are we giving implicit permission to engage in sex? It all depends on our message. It seems to make sense for our schools to give information to kids. That is their job— to inform and educate about the world around us. It is also important for kids to get the message at home about what their family culture and values are all about. Kids, if taught well at home by modeling, will pick up the values there. We definitely want them to gain values from other sources as well, but schools have a job of teaching the facts as they are, as objectively as possible, so that the kids can put them to work in their own respective value systems.

The SIECUS (Sexuality Information and Education Council of the United States) Report tells us that using a condom is more than 10,000 times safer than not using a condom during intercourse. Also that condoms are 98% effective when used correctly—with some reports indicating they are 100% effective. The average failure rate for condoms is 12%, reflective of people who do not use them properly or do not use them every time they have intercourse. Laboratory tests show that neither sperm, which has a diameter of 3 microns (0.003mm), nor STD-causing organisms, which are a quarter to a ninth the size of sperm, can penetrate an intact latex condom.

The SIECUS Report also tells us that condom use substantially reduces the risk of HIV transmission. A study in the <u>New England Journal of Medicine</u> observed partners for 20 months where one was HIV-positive and the other was HIV-negative. Findings were that HIV-negative partners did not become infected when condoms were used consistently and correctly, but 10% became infected (12 of 122) when condoms were used inconsistently. Another study reported in <u>The Journal of Aquired Immune Deficiency Syndromes</u> showed that in a similar group, 3% (2 of 171) who consistently and correctly used condoms became HIV-infected, whereas 15% (8 of 55) who used condoms inconsistently, became infected. Another study in the <u>American Journal of Epidemiology</u> observed female partners of sero-positive men (HIV-positive) and showed that inconsistent or no condom use during vaginal and anal intercourse was associated with HIV infection.

Abstinence is the only 100% effective prevention against STD's, but of those who report abstinence as their contraception method, 26% become pregnant each year, and 80% of all people have intercourse at least once by the age of 20.

Homosexuality (Gay & Lesbian):

Yes, we do have to look at the "other" kind of sexual behavior. Homosexuality has been present in our western culture since at least the time of the ancient Greeks. The questions that most frequently come up about homosexuality include: Is this behavior learned or innate? Is it normal or abnormal? Is it sinful?

Learned or innate: It makes sense that there are some people, both male and female, who have had traumatic experiences of a sexual nature that tend to turn them off to sexual behavior with people of the opposite sex, and that they have learned to be more comfortable with same sex relationships. There also are studies that would point out that some individuals have clearly identified a sexual preference for the same sex from a very early age, seemingly independent of later sexual experiences. Thus it would appear that in some people, a propensity to be attracted to the same sex may be present from birth. In others, the attraction may be learned from life experience.

Normal or Abnormal: We have to go back to our earlier model of four different notions of normality (statistical, ideal, healthy, process).

If we look at statistics, we find that there are many people in our society who have homosexual proclivities and/or lifestyles. They may be in the minority, but they are clearly a significant percentage of our culture. If we want to say that, because they are not in the majority, statistically, they are abnormal, from a statistical point of view, we would also have to say that Catholics, Asian-Americans, Jews, Italian-Americans, Libertarians, certain politicians and many others are abnormal.

In earlier times, when we were needing to people the planet, when people died young, when social security meant having enough kids to take care of you in your old age, it was ideal to have families and intimate relationships that resulted in having children. In our present era when more people on the planet is not necessarily good, it does not appear to be abnormal from an ideal perspective of normal to have relationships of intimacy that do not result in additional children on the planet. This does not mean that gay couples should not have children, but the preponderance of children in such relationships are already present in the world, and come to these families from previous relationships or through adoption.

If we look at normal from the perspective of health, I would say that the health of a relationship usually depends on how respectively and lovingly people treat one another in such a relationship. Until a recent Supreme Court ruling, in some states, homosexual relationships were not legally able to be bound in a marriage ceremony. Those people who stayed together most often did so because they are committed to one another, not because they are bound legally and financially to do so. Normality from the perspective of health would have to be judged on the same basis that heterosexual relationships are judged. Healthy love is based not on power, but on giving, and not on control, but on respect.

Let's look at the normality of homosexuality on the basis of process. It would appear to me that the fundamental question in this life is the issue of how we learn to love. Most of the religions of the world approach this question in some form or another. The process of homosexual behavior would appear to be a process of finding a way to love and to be intimate in some meaningful way to another individual. It allows the individual to expand beyond oneself to "otherness" rather than to "selfness". Love has to be expanded to "otherness". That is the nature of love, to get beyond the self and think and care for others.

Is it Sinful?: The nature of **sin**, in my understanding is that it **is self-directed**. If that is true, then any sexual behavior that is entirely self-directed, is potentially sinful. If heterosexual behavior is non-caring for the other person and only for personal gratification, it is far from favorable behavior. On the other hand, if homosexual behavior is loving and demonstrating caring and concern for the partner, perhaps that is not sinful, assuming that it is discreet and not modeling inappropriate intimacy, as any sexual behavior should be.

In the movie, "Papillon", with Dustin Hoffman and Steve McQueen, there was a scene where Hoffman was asked if he would blame McQueen, if he confessed in his solitary confinement cell, about who had helped him by putting fresh coconut in his daily swill rations (Hoffman had done so.). Hoffman answered, **"Blame is for God and small children."**

Among the parents we have seen, the **major concerns** about a son or daughter taking on a gay lifestyle usually includes the foreseeable pain that that child will encounter. A rewarding lifestyle is not limited to heterosexuals, but parents know that a gay person will often encounter prejudice, and that the finding of a satisfactory gay partner in our society is not always an easy task. There is also the fact that in some gay relationships, grandchildren are just not in the picture, a very important item in many parents' lives. Surely, in some gay relationships, a previous relationship has allowed for children to be raised by gay couples, but in the teen group, this prospect is not easily foreseeable. So, we go back to the basic job of parents, that of teacher and protector. The parent teaches how to love and how to survive. A gay lifestyle tends to jump out at both those issues. Can this child expect to form a lasting intimate relationship, and can this child survive in the world?

How do parents most effectively approach the child who is entertaining the notion that he/she may be gay? Coming out like gangbusters at the kid is probably not the best idea. If one wants to help a child with issues of self-identity, which is fairly common in these teen years, though not always in the arena of sexual identity, the most effective approach would likely be to listen and be receptive to the young person. Rushing the child off to a counselor or psychiatrist without sitting down to listen to the feelings of the child is not a great idea. It might be a good idea, if after talking it over, both of you think it might help to sort things out. The important thing to let your kid know is that this is a decision that does not have to be made immediately. It is one that the kid can take all the time that he needs to think over. Also, we have seen kids make decisions about their sexual identity based on very minor events, many of which have nothing whatsoever to do with gender, masculinity or femininity, so it is important to allow them enough time to thoroughly examine the issues that they see themselves as facing.

We have tried to look in this chapter at sexual behavior, its ramifications, its variations, its consequences and complications. I am sure that we have just scratched the surface, particularly in regard to transgender issues, though many of the issues discussed above would also apply to them.

Pearls For Parents:

1) It is a must at some point early on to talk to your kids about sexual behavior, including birth control, sexually transmitted diseases, pregnancy, and peer pressure.

2) A young teen may find it embarrassing at first to talk about sex, but frankly they are going to cue off the parents' anxiety about talking about this stuff. If you are reluctant, they will avoid the topic as well. You prefer them to get straight information from you rather that distorted information from their peers.

3) The best way to push a kid in a direction that you do not want him to go is to insist that he do it your way. "Seeding" an idea is usually much more effective. You plant the seed, nourish the idea (but in a subtle manner) and let it grow. When it has developed, the kid will like the idea, because he will think it was his in the first place.

4) It is important to trust your kids, but everyone, including a kid you trust, will make bad choices some of the time. That is how we learn best—from our mistakes. How many times did you have to find out something for yourself, even after your parents told you? For this reason it is important to limit the number of situations, as best you can, that will allow your kid to make bad or dumb choices. The less the opportunities to screw up, the fewer number of screwups there will be, good kids though they may be.

5) Remember that the biggest sex organ is the brain.

6) Alcohol and drugs alter one's ability to make sensible decisions.

Examples of sexual behavior with **some risk (possibly safe)** include: French kissing (wet kissing), vaginal intercourse with a condom, anal intercourse with a condom, fellatio (blow job) that stops before ejaculation into the mouth, cunnilingus (tongue in woman's vagina), and urine on unbroken skin. Examples of **un-safe sex** include: vaginal or anal intercourse without a condom, semen or urine in mouth, sharing sex toys, sharing IV drug needles, blood contact, and oral/anal contact.

<u>**Last but not least, get your child immunized for Human Papillomavirus at an early age!! Speak with the child's pediatrician about this by the time he/she is 11 years old, or if beyond 11, ASAP!! Cancer can show up decades after the original infection.**</u>

Resources:

Classic Movies:

"Do You Know The Muffin Man?" (Pam Dawber, John Shea)

"The Accused" (Jodie Foster, Kelly McGillis)

"The Summer of '42" (Jennifer O'Neal)

"A Walk to Remember"

"Brooklyn"

"Shirley Valentine"

Organizations:

1) CDC (Center for Disease Control and Prevention) www.cdc.gov/std; www.cdc.gov.cancer; www.cdc.gov.hpv/

2) American Sexual Health Association www.ashasexualhealth.org

3) Planned Parenthood usually has an office in most fair-sized communities. They offer information on prevention of disease and pregnancy, as well as choices for those who wish to complete a pregnancy safely. www.plannedparenthood.org

4) Lifescript www.lifescript.com/stds

5) National Cancer Institute www.cancer.gov

Chapter 8
RELIGION AND SPIRITUALITY

"Glory be to God for dappled things—
For skies of couple-colour as a brinded cow;
For rose-moles all in stipple upon trout that swim;
—Gerard Manley Hopkins "Pied Beauty"

From earliest times, mankind has been aware of a non-material or spiritual element to its makeup. Some dispute it, but every culture from primitive man to modern times has a tradition of looking to some form of higher power or powers to understand another aspect of our purpose here on earth. The very fact that humans have the ability to abstract from their circumstances and reflect on themselves gives rise to speculation about the spiritual side of our nature. Thus, in spite of the fact that some individuals, for whatever their reasons, choose to ignore or to deny this aspect of humanity, enough of us have accepted this concept that we will address the spiritual needs of teens and religion as a legitimate point on which to focus in this chapter.

Families tend to carry traditions, and one of these is commonly a particular religious affiliation or set of values. Sometimes it is no particular religious affiliation, but the family's set of values still comes through. Religious and spiritual values often develop gradually, much as Kohlberg described moral development, discussed in the chapter on adolescent development. A young child's notions of religion are pretty much what he is told. Children tend to accept what adults tell them. They readily tend to believe in the magical. When the teen years start, the more complicated questions begin. Notions become more abstract. What appear to be inconsistencies or contradictions arise. What some adults accept on faith or consider to be "mysteries" not to be fathomed by our limited natures, teens tend to question. One might say at this stage in their development, that it is a questioning stage.

Questioning religious tenets is not necessarily a bad thing. Most followers of religion believe in a supreme being who gives mankind the freedom to choose between right and wrong. Think of it. If one does not have the freedom to choose, then we are no different than other animals who strictly follow their natures without a second thought. If one does not question what one is told (other than in a life and death situation, where taking orders from someone in charge is paramount) the individual loses his individuality and follows the pack. He loses his freedom to choose what he really believes.

Extremes: All the way back to early history, the Greeks talked about extremes. Heraclitus believed that everything in nature was constantly changing, that nothing remained the same from moment to moment. If one looked at a river, it was never the same river, because different water was in the place one looked. Parmenides, on the other hand, believed that nothing changed, that it was always the same. This river was always this river. It took Aristotle, much later, to arrive at a solution. The matter (or material cause) of the river changed all the time, but the form (formal cause) of the river remained constant. Whether or not we accept these rather simplified explanations is not the issue. The fact is that neither extreme is a likely solution, and the answer sometimes lies somewhere in the middle. Aristotle himself described the "golden mean" as a means of achieving a sensible way of living. By this, he espoused living somewhere in the mean or middle, between extremes.

The world is full of people who all think somewhat differently. Part of this is the result of growing up in different cultures, whether national cultures or family cultures. Part of it is the result of where individuals are developmentally, whether because of age, training, education, environment or personal history. Religious problems often arise when these differences are not accepted, or when economics and religion clash. The problems in

Northern Ireland, for example, are not all differences in religion between Catholics and Protestants, but economic. Who will get the scarce jobs available? This is not all of the equation, but is certainly part of it.

Extremes can be a problem for teens, because they are frequently just coming into the time of their lives when they are conceptualizing more clearly about abstract ideas. They have sometimes not yet had the life experience to weigh the practical issues that allow for considering the way others may view these ideas. Religion is certainly one area where people can take extreme stands; some such stands can tend to alienate the individual from his peers. At the same time, it is important for young people to know where their moral "bottom line" is, that is, just how far they will go to gain peer acceptance, and sometimes it is important to take a firm stand for what one believes in. It is a fine line, much like the one that parents have to develop in knowing when to back off being a buddy to your kid and again taking the role of manager or warden. As parents learn, it is often a process of learning by trial and error, and kids often have to learn the same way. Thus it behooves parents to have patience and to oversee the mistakes of their kids, hoping to guide them in their better choices the next time around.

Values: In order to impart religious values in our kids, it all comes back to what we teach them and how we do it. From the earlier chapter on communication, we learned that the best way to teach is by example, and there is no better way to teach moral and spiritual values than by modeling what we believe. Sometimes the best lesson for us as parents to model, is how we deal with our mistakes. If our kids respect us, they will respect our values. Even if they make choices to do otherwise, these values will be ingrained in them, and they will come back to them sooner or later. If we model for them how we deal with our mistakes, they will have an idea about how to deal with their own.

Secondary Benefits: Spirituality, morality and religion certainly have their primary benefits, but involvement in a church or temple definitely has its secondary gains as well. Many churches and temples have youth groups and offer numerous activities for young people. Such groups often offer educational opportunities and discussion groups within a framework that feels safe for kids to explore their doubts or concerns without feeling threatened about their faith. They offer support, relieving anxiety about stressful events. They provide companionship and healthy relationships among their peers. They provide recreational outlets that are generally safe and healthy at a time when the youth is trying to complicate his/her life to make it exciting (as we are trying to simplify ours to make it tolerable), and they give the kid a sense of acceptance and belonging.

Not all secondary benefits of religion come from youth groups. Regardless of whether such opportunities exist, there is usually a sense of belonging that is important to young people. There is a sense of direction to "otherness", by which I mean a looking to the needs and concerns of others, not just of oneself. There is a sense of clarity about ethics and morals, about what is right and wrong, good and bad, and often a sense of comfort in making proper choices. It also offers teens the opportunity to meet others of the opposite sex in a setting that offers healthy outlets to explore their growing identities.

Pitfalls and Problems: One of the problems that may arise for anyone who is immersed in one's faith is the issue of **magical thinking**. I am not referring to the idea of miracles or divine intervention. Certainly such things may occur, but if one depends on them as a matter of course, problems arise. Saint Augustine is supposed to have said, "Pray like everything depends on God, but work like everything depends on you." This is not a bad practical sentiment whether one is Christian, Jewish, Muslim, B'hai, Hindu, Shinto, Buddhist, or whatever.

Some sects tend to focus a great deal on the negative. There is a great deal of **emphasis on punishment**. The problem with this is that studies have found that the best reinforcement for good behavior is reward or encouragement or positive feeling when the good behavior is achieved, and punishment is not as effective, though at times it may be necessary. Teenagers may at first be frightened about fire and brimstone, but after awhile, when the lightning bolts have not arrived as promised, the opportunity is lost. Whether or not an eternity of shoveling coal is awaiting some of us or not, most teens are not spending much of their time speculating about their demise. They still feel physically great, and have difficulty conceptualizing their mortality. In the meantime, focusing on the negative may lose them entirely.

Rejection by others because of one's faith can be very real, and very painful. It certainly happens. It may be that it helps the kids to examine carefully what they believe and accept. Sometimes it means we accept what we cannot change with as good a spirit as we can muster. Sometimes it may lead to dialogue and acceptance of others at a particular level.

Some parents have concerns about what happens when rejection does not occur, and **interfaith romantic relationships** begin. This can be very touchy in some families and can be a very fine line to walk. Remember—many relationships in the teen years are extremely intense, but also can be fairly short-lived. The nature of relationships at this age is to explore the nature of the opposite sex, to learn who and what one likes and does not like, and to move on relatively quickly between relationships, while treating others with respect and building one's own character in the process. The best way that I know of to make sure that two teens stay together for a long time is to tell them not to. The main thing that parents must do during these times of dating is to make sure, as best as can be done, that the opportunity for inappropriate behaviors is minimized. As good as intentions may be and as good as the kids may be, given the right circumstances and the heat of the moment, anything can happen, and I do mean sex. I have discussed sex and sexuality in another chapter, but it should be said that sex definitely changes relationships and intensifies them. It makes the natural dating shifts among teens more difficult, once this kind of intimacy begins.

Cults: There are several meanings of the word cult in the dictionary. The word can refer to a particular system of religious worship, with reference to its rites and ceremonies. It can refer to an instance of great veneration of a person, ideal or thing (like a cult of Napolean or of the devil), or a group or sect bound together by devotion to or veneration of the same thing, person or ideal, etc. Other similar meanings exist, but these days, when we think of cults, we often envision, at its worst, a predatory group ready to take advantage of naive and needy teenagers or young adults, and who take them into their midst, preventing contact with families until the youth is thoroughly brainwashed and unwilling to return to any meaningful contact with others outside this group.

Clearly, as with anything, there are different degrees of cult activity. Again, our job as parents includes trying to prepare our kids for the world outside, and there are predatory people out there. How do we make our kids safe? As one person confided in me years ago, she believed there are two types of parents in this regard, the wallbuilders and the immunizers. Her theory was that there are those parents who build walls to try to keep all the bad out, and there are those parents who try to inoculate their kids with a little bit of bad, bit by bit (like someone who gets live polio vaccine) to introduce them to the "disease" or "badness" in such a way that they learn to handle it a little at a time. She felt that those parents who built walls did not prepare their kids for the real world, and when they got out past the walls, they were much more susceptible to falling prey to the "badness" than those who had been immunized. Even those who stay within the walls may begin to notice cracks in those walls. When the bricks in those walls begin to crack, it is not too long afterward that the walls begin to deteriorate and fall. Then there is more of a likelihood of the whole system of thought falling apart. I am not saying that this is the answer to concerns about cult behavior, but perhaps if we start early in helping our kids to ask questions, to evaluate what we say or do and how we do it, to looking at the world as it is and not protecting too much, they may be less susceptible to black and white, all or none thinking.

The other aspect of susceptibility to cult behavior besides the naiveté that may exist, is the neediness or dependency that such predatory individuals pick up on very quickly. Those young people who have been raised being afraid to make a move without consulting an authority, who are raised with a strong sense of rigidity in their parental figures, are more likely to be coming into their rebellion at their parents with an unawareness of their sense of dependence on yet another level of authority, namely the cult leaders. Again, this is where a history of a healthy questioning of authority comes in handy. I certainly don't mean that parents should get into a half-hour or more conference with a kid on the disputation of every parental decision, but the kid should know that, if not now, perhaps in the future, there is room for further consideration of the kid's point of view, even if the rules aren't changed, and they should also know that there may be times when a parent may change his mind or at least reconsider. They should also learn that circumstances may well change how a parent considers things.

When kids get caught up in cults, it can be a heartbreaking experience for families. Whether it happens to be a situation where the kid gets caught up with following a religious figure whose followers practice isolation from other "non-followers", or is caught up with an anti-religious movement such as a Satanic cult, family pain is usually the end result. There are some things one can do. If a child is going through a significant personality change and is alienating from family and friends, if performance deteriorates, whether in the family, at work or at school, and if there is a sudden shift in values or belief system with a rejection of former beliefs and values, one should begin to suspect the presence of a cult phenomenon in the child's experience. There may be an excessive amount of time involved with the new group and the group may begin to control the kid's decisions, so that his ability to think critically becomes affected. In Satanic cults, there may be pre-occupation with death or suicidal thoughts, cruelty to animals, changing sexual attitudes, drug or alcohol abuse, withdrawal and secretiveness. The kid's sense of humor may be lost, and previous affiliations with the family religion are frequently lost. There is often an obsession with heavy metal music and themes of violence, death, rape and demonism. Satanic symbols (666—pentagrams—inverted crosses) may decorate the room, books, T-shirts, or be worn as jewelry.

This book cannot go into all the details of how to deal with cult activity, but there are many resources available to help families deal with the aftermath of cult involvement. I will list some of these resources at the end of this chapter.

Birth Control: Another sensitive issue for many people, particularly Catholics. What do we tell our teenagers about birth control? Sex is and always has been a struggle for adolescents, but since the 60's and the "sexual revolution", it has been more a concern for parents, who have a natural inclination to protect their kids and who see an increase in the amount of overt sexual activity among young people.

As always, the use of artificial devices to control pregnancy is often combined with the prevention of disease, and this issue is discussed further in the chapter on sexuality, but the overall issue of birth control whether by use of condom or diaphragm, hormone control (birth control pills), or other means (withdrawal before ejaculation, spermicides, IUD, etc.) is something that responsible parents of teens these days need to address.

There are a number of moral issues to be addressed here. First, are we giving permission to have sex by discussing and/or giving permission to use birth control if sexual behavior is engaged in? Secondly, are we just hiding our heads in the sand by not wanting to talk about these issues with our kids. Thirdly, is birth control itself moral? It may be that parents themselves do not agree with the notion of birth control and would prefer that their children not use it at all either. That does not take away the responsibility to inform their kids adequately about the issues in this day and age.

Present day moral thought and most religions teach us that the **human conscience is the barometer of moral decisions**. In the wake of the holocaust, we can no longer afford to delegate our consciences to our leaders and others who would have us think that they know better. We must make decisions for ourselves, and whether we like it or not, our teenage children will do the same, as we did with our parents. Thus we must help them to arrive at decisions with the most information we have at hand, since people with the most information have the opportunity to make the best decisions.

Let us look for a moment at the **historical context** of how women were valued in the Old Testament and in the early days of the Christian church, and to some extent in parts of the world today. Women were revered as fertile child-brides who would usually be betrothed to older mature men to bear and raise their children, and as they grew older, revered as mothers. They did not have the opportunity to make decisions in the households of import except for the domestic area. They were protected and guarded as the ones capable of begetting and raising children and heirs. The role of sex was closely guarded as a means of procreation, and people tended to die off rather early in those days. The early church fathers lived in this era and continued this teaching. At the same time there was a movement referred in the early Christian church called the "Manichean heresy", which essentially said that everything of the body (the material part of a person) was evil, and everything of the spiritual side was good. Therefore anything to do with sex was inherently evil. This kind of thinking carried over into other areas of thought, and over the centuries, the tradition in the early church was that sex itself was a threat to salvation and had to be held in check, only to be used for a singular purpose, the procreation of children. Eventually the addition of the notion of the education of children entered the picture as well. Because women were not considered equals to men for many centuries, the ideas of unity and sharing, tenderness and affection, and the notion that a close sexual union between men and women might be a means of salvation by teaching the true meaning of love, took until a more modern time to become a consideration.

In addition to this imperative in the early church to not do the unthinkable (thwart women's procreative role), the development in the 17th century of a different notion of "natural law", namely the notion espoused by Rousseau in his "Social Contract", was born. Rousseau strongly stated that we should go "back to nature" and an almost romantic idealism about the purity of the natural was set in motion. Professor Frederick E. Flynn, who taught ethics at St. Thomas College in St. Paul, Minnesota, described the distortion of the notion of natural law as stemming partly from a confusion of this notion of Rousseau and the notion of natural law as espoused by Thomas Aquinas. Aquinas, he says, considered natural law to be a sharing of God's eternal law, but the way that man shares in this immutable law is to use what God has given him to understand the world around him, namely his ability to reason, to arrive at what God's eternal law is. Therefore Aquinas would consider natural law to be "universal human reason" or that which most reasonable men would arrive at in making decisions about their universe. Thus, Professor Flynn would say that since man builds domiciles, bridges, roads, wears clothes, cooks his food, etc., he is constantly thwarting nature, but is using his God-given intelligence to do so, and in the process is imitating God, or working in his image. Professor Flynn would go on to say that the purpose of sex may be the procreation and education of children, but to properly educate children, one must have the time and energy to do so. If one has children indiscriminately, one will not have either the time or the energy, nor the money to educate children properly in this day and age. Thus Flynn would say that it is perfectly within the realm of natural law to improve on nature, using our reason, by preventing an overabundance of children which cannot be properly supported nor taught, much as we might improve on nature by planting a garden to raise a large crop of hybrid vegetables that would help us to feed our family. In an agrarian society, many children were needed for social security. When the parents grew up, the children continued to run the farm and support the aging parents. The world is different now, and this tends not to be the case—another reason not to have so many children.

You may ask, "What does all this have to do with teenage sex?" The answer is that we do not operate in a vacuum. How we approach sex and sexuality and the notion of birth control is going to rub off on our children. If we have a sense that birth control is inherently evil, rather than a means to sensibly and responsibly raise our families and respectfully love our spouses without the frustrations and uncertainties of "Vatican roulette", as the rhythm method in the Catholic world is so fondly referred to, then this will enter into our dealings with our kids about these same issues. Now premarital sex among teens is not the same as marital sex, and I am not recommending it, but whether I or any parents recommend teen sex has nothing to do with whether it will occur or not. More about this in the chapter on sexuality.

I do not pretend to make this chapter a comprehensive statement on religion in teenage years. Such a topic is much too complex to be contained in a book such as this. I do, however, want to impart some ideas that I, as a mental health professional, do see as helpful in this population.

Pearls For Parents:

1) Kids like to rattle their parents. Just look at typical ten year old "toilet talk". They like to say things that they themselves might have been shocked at a year or two earlier. Now they can talk openly about "shitting" and "burping", "farting" and "peuking". Teens do it in a little more subtle fashion, but not much. They may make some comment about religion for the shock value, or just as another means of declaring their independence.

2) When teens ask questions about religion, don't necessarily take the questions at face value. Look for the underlying question, and see if you can answer that one too. It may start up a nice dialogue that will help the kid to answer an underlying question that is really concerning him.

3) Encourage conversation in the family about values and religion. Kids may be surprised about what you think and believe. They may be assuming a great deal, based on much earlier notions from their childhood. Allow them to have their questions and perhaps doubts, but give them some alternatives to consider and think about and maybe come back to those same questions later.

4) Remember that decisions that are made as young children—that are reasonable in a child's mind, because of the developmental stage—are often not reconsidered and changed to what might be more appropriate decisions for an older person at a different developmental stage. Re-examination of these ideas,

including conceptions of parental figures, is important in the light of new thinking abilities as a child gets older. In my practice I frequently see adults who still view themselves based on notions they developed about themselves as very young children. It is natural for a child, for example, to accept the fact that if he is being abused by an adult, and, assuming that that he thinks adults know what is right, he is likely to accept the notion that he is bad and deserves to be abused. Such a notion can continue to be held by a child well into teen and adult life, influencing decisions about behavior and self concept.

5) It has been said that adolescence is the recapitulation of the early formative years of childhood, but on a more global scale. Thus we see the 18 month old child toddling off from the mother's side to explore things in the room, only to repeatedly toddle back to mom to check that she is still there, and then off to explore again. The teen does this, but on a community level instead of in the room. Thus it is good that the teen questions ideas of religion, because it gives him a chance to leave the mother's side for a while and to wander back and forth, finding out what he really believes. Most of the time it will be encrusted with the values that he has been raised with. It does give the teen a chance to develop his sense of freedom and to re-examine the notions that he learned as a child to see how they fit his life as a teen and later as an adult.

Resources:

Books:

1) <u>The Bible</u>

2) <u>The Responsible Christian</u> by Reverend Vincent E. Rush 1984 Loyola University Press Chicago, IL 60657

3) <u>Mind Control and the Psychology of Totalism</u>

by Robert Jay Lifton

4) <u>What Modern Catholics Think About Birth Control</u> *A New Symposium* edited by William Birmingham A Signet Book published by The New American Library New York 1964 (may be out of print)

5) <u>Captive Hearts, Captive Minds: Freedom and Recovery from Cults and Abusive Relationships</u> by Madeleine Landau Tobias and Janja Lalich—Alameda CA—Hunter House, 1994

6) <u>Combating Cult Mind Control</u> by Steve Hassan - Rochester VT Park Street Press, 1988

7) <u>Cults: What Parents Should Know</u> by Joan C. Ross and Michael D. Langone—Secaucus, NJ—Lyle Stuart, 1989

8) <u>Cults in Our Midst</u> by Margaret Thaler Singer with Janja Lalich San Francisco, CA: Jossey-Bass, 1995

9) <u>Influence: The New Psychology of Modern Persuasion</u> by Robert Cialdini—New York: Quill, 1984

10) <u>The Screwtape Letters</u> (Letters from a senior to a junior devil) by C.S. Lewis

11) Sidhartha by Herman Hesse

Classic Movies:

1) "Elmer Gantry"

2) "Inherit The Wind"

3) "Oh, God"

4) "A Walk to Remember"

5) "A Man For All Seasons"

6) "The Mission"

7) "Babette's Feast"

8) "The Shawshank Redemption"

9) "On The Waterfront"

Chapter 9
MENTAL HEALTH IN ADOLESCENTS

"Here's the smell of the blood still: all the perfumes
of Arabia will not sweeten this little hand."
—Lady Macbeth in "Macbeth"by William Shakespeare

Normality: Looking at normal from the health perspective is not all that different from other perspectives. People always want to know if their teenagers' behaviors are "normal". We'll review again the meaning of the word and concept "normal".

As we saw in Chapter II, normal can be seen from at least four different perspectives, which we will review:

1) Normal as **statistical**—statistical normal is what most people do in a given situation. If 95% of the population sleeps 8 hours per night, that is normal. If 95% of Lemmings rush to their deaths into the ocean once every 5-10 years, that is normal Lemming behavior. However if **all** Lemmings rushed to their deaths, that would be the end of Lemmings, so some of them stay home and let the others go rushing off. Some of them choose *abnormal* behavior. Thomas Edison only slept a few hours each night and caught catnaps during the day. That made him *abnormal* but that was not necessarily bad. Thus we see that statistical normal is a way we stack ourselves up against the rest of the population, but not something to which we need to strongly adhere.

2) Normal as **ideal (utopian)**—some people view normal as what is optimal or best, even if it is unattainable. Sigmund Freud, for example, would have classified many behaviors that would be considered statistically normal, as abnormal, not that Freud was correct about all things, but let us also look at some religious tenets. Masturbation is quite common among adolescent boys, but some would say that this is not normal, and in this sense of the word, I believe they are using the concept of normal as ideal from their perspective.

3) Normal as **healthy**—using the example above, some people may think that masturbation for young boys is not healthy. We often think of health and normal synonymously. If a person has a cancer in his lung, he is not thought of as normal in one sense. At least he doesn't have a normal lung, and if he has heart disease, he doesn't have a normal heart. He isn't normal. If a person is schizophrenic and hears voices that tell him to hurt people, he isn't normal. He has an abnormality in his brain. An adolescent male who is masturbating would appear to have healthy genital organs. The question for some people would be whether or not the behavior is healthy brain behavior.

4) Normal as **process or development**—if a two year old has an accident and wets his pants, that is pretty well considered normal by most people. If a sixteen year old has an accident and wets his pants, it is considered a bit unusual, and probably as not normal. It is developmentally normal for the two year old to have such an accident, but a sixteen year old usually has his sphincter under control by this time. Thus what may be perfectly normal under some circumstances is not under others, depending on the state of development of any given process. For a 39 yr. old man to stand for hours and primp in front of a mirror is a very different matter than that of a 14 year old girl.

5) Yet another concept of normal has recently come to my awareness. While talking to two different patients, I was discussing the concept of normal, and each of these people reminded that their behavior was "normal for me", or, in other words,

normal in the context of their usual behavior as they knew themselves. Thus, ultimately, people need to make a decision about whether they like themselves the way they are, or whether they want to make some changes to make life easier or better, or at least different for themselves.

Psychiatric Disorders:

There are basically eight main types of psychiatric disorders:
1) Psychosis
2) Neurosis
3) Personality Disorder
4) Psychosomatic Disorder
5) Substance Abuse
6) Impulse Control Disorder
7) Developmental Disorder
8) Other organic impairment

Naturally things aren't quite as simple as this, and there are other ways to classify these and other disorders, but it gives us a skeleton to work with. We have learned over the years that many mental illnesses are often the result of changes in the brain. Sometimes these changes are the result of habits developed over the years, sometimes not. Sometimes they are just waiting like a computer virus in our genes, ready to be activated by something not in our control. Let's look at these general categories.

Psychosis: Essentially this means that an individual has a problem, some or all of the time, sorting out what is real from what is not real. For example, someone may have the notion that he or she can read other people's thoughts, or can receive special messages from the radio or television. Most people are aware that this is not within the power of people to do. Yet this person believes it with all his/her conviction. If it persists, it is an ongoing psychotic manifestation; if it is short-lived, as with an acute hallucinogenic drug intoxication, it is still a form of psychosis, but not necessarily a permanent one. Psychoses often occur as a result of some biochemical impairment, sometimes genetically passed on.

Neurosis: People with neuroses are in touch with reality, but are influenced a great deal by anxiety. Neurosis refers to those problems that have their basis in anxiety such as anxiety states, depression of certain types, obsessive thoughts, phobias, etc.

People with anxiety-related disorders may feel as though they are crazy or going crazy, but if they could find a means of relieving the anxious feelings, their thinking process is very clear and without a distortion of reality.

Personality Disorders: These are basically habit patterns of living that are maladaptive, developed over time, that tend not to bother the owner as much as the people around him/her. The pattern is often learned by happenstance or accident as certain behaviors elicit other behaviors in others that end up serving a purpose or satisfying a need. Examples of this would be: histrionic behavior (like on a stage—exaggerated) that gets a desired response, passive-aggressive behavior (aggressive, but in a passive way such as doing things very slowly so they don't get done or breaking things purposely because the task ordered to be done was onerous). We all engage in some of these kinds of behaviors, but when they become a way of life, they are often characterized as personality disorders.

Psychosomatic Illness: This is real illness, but caused or aggravated by the stress of psychological issues. Examples are ulcers, high blood pressure, irritable bowel, headache, etc. They are clearly stress-related.

Substance abuse: Abuse of alcohol, prescription drugs, street drugs, or other available chemicals such as glue, gasoline, paint, etc. Sometimes it leads to addiction (which means the body develops a craving for the substance) and sometimes to habituation (which means there is a psychological craving for the substance).

Impulse Control Disorders: Some individuals have difficulty containing their impulses, such as gambling, sexual behavior, stealing, lying, setting fires, or just keeping their rage under control. Difficult though they may find this to control, they are still responsible for the behaviors.

Developmental Disorders: Some individuals are afflicted with difficulties from an early age. Other than mental retardation, which most people recognize in people who appear "slower" than others mentally, there are also other disorders that might make individuals look "different". Some people have specific learning disorders, making it difficult for them to read or do math, or express themselves through writing. Others have motor skill problems or have communication disorders making expressive or receptive language difficult. Others have difficulty forming the words for speech. The more severe developmental disorders lie in the autism spectrum and can be very severe, looking to the lay observer like mental retardation. They can also be milder forms of autism such as Asperger's Disorder, where the individual looks pretty normal, but has difficulty with changes in routine, tends to think very concretely, and has difficulty with peer social interactions.

Organic Impairment means that there is something physically not working as it should in the brain. By not working as it should, I mean, not as most other peoples' brains work to do the usual day to day operations without a hitch. There are some people, like Thomas Edison, whose brain may not have worked like other peoples', but we would not consider his functioning impaired, but perhaps improved by the difference, or he may have overcompensated for his difficulties by finding other better ways to get things done, given his particular biology. People who have impairment that interferes are those who have conditions such as seizures, which interfere with consciousness, or such as processing difficulties in the brain like attention deficit disorder (often accompanied by hyperactivity), or specific learning difficulties such as dyslexia (inability to read in a functional way). Some if not all of the Developmental disorders clearly have an organic basis.

Is all adolescence an unbalanced state? Certainly many adolescents struggle with erratic behavior, but marked adolescent turmoil reflects deviant rather than normative adjustment. If we look at this time in a teenager's life, it reflects back on similar developmental issues dealt with at a much younger age, and we can much better understand it. At age 2 or thereabouts, a child goes through an individuation stage of development where the child insists on his ability to say "no". This is often referred to as the "terrible two's". It is a time when a child first begins to realize at a very primitive level, that he is actually separate from his mother and can do things other than what she wants him to do. The child is beginning to have a sense of a separate identity, and in order to understand it, has to practice what it means by saying "no" and doing something that he wants rather than what he is told. Also at the toddler stage we see children leave mother's side to go off short distances to explore, but they frequently return to mom's side to "check in" and then go off on another short jaunt.

In looking at teenagers' behavior, we need to look at similar struggles with identity and individuation, and with exploration of the world, but both on a much more expanded scale. Now they are done out of sight and out of earshot. They are done out in the world, mainly with their peer group, a developmentally "normal" occurrence for a teenager. If we look at various studies of "normal" teenagers, "the data clearly indicate that adolescents in general are no more likely than other segments of the population to display features of psychological maladjustment." However, "accumulating evidence suggests that symptoms of psychological disturbance warrant as much concern and professional attention in adolescents as they do in adults."

Most common psychological problems seen in adolescent mental health practices: Probably the most common problems I have seen in my practice over the past 30 years are as follows. I will first list them and then try to talk a little about each one.

Depression
Anxiety/ Post-traumatic Stress Disorder
Impulse Control Disorders

Obsessive-Compulsive Disorder
Eating Disorders

Other concerns and disorders which present and are troublesome, but perhaps not as frequent as the above. I will address some of the more common and more troublesome.

Schizophrenia
Developmental Disorders
Tourette's Disorder
Personality Disorders
Bipolar (Manic-Depressive) Disorder
Dissociative Disorders

There are also very troubling issues that come up for teens that may be major or minor for the people around them, but can be very traumatic for them. Love for a teen is just as intense, though perhaps more short-lived, as for an adult. Then there is the often traumatic issue both for the teen as well as for the rest of the family when a teen begins to sense that perhaps he/she is a homosexual. Depending on one's point of view, these may be or may not be viewed as unhealthy or "abnormal", and some families handle the situation with great patience and forbearance while others are blown away and the situation sometimes gets out of hand.

Let us begin to look specifically at some of the various individual problem areas:

Depression: The first thing we have to do is define depression. There are many people who go around saying, "I'm so depressed.", but many of these people are not depressed, but rather are unhappy with their given circumstances. There is not a good word in our language for depression. It is a disturbance of mood of long-standing duration that interferes with our ability to perform our day to day tasks of living. It manifests itself in different ways. In young people, it often presents as surly, angry, irritable behavior that is often self-defeating. In older people, it may be more inwardly directed. However, when an individual begins to experience a number of the following symptoms, one can be sure that the depression has gotten to the point where biochemical changes have occurred in the brain's processing of information that need to be reversed in order for the person to adequately take charge of his/her own mood once again. These symptoms include:

a) diminished energy

b) difficulty concentrating and with memory

c) sad or discouraged mood (sometimes a sense of hopelessness)

d) low self-esteem

e) increased crying

f) insomnia or other difficulty with sleep (difficulty getting to sleep, staying asleep, early awakening) —or

g) excessive sleep

h) loss of appetite sometimes with weight loss —or

i) sometimes overeating (maybe getting comfort in food)

j) difficulty getting going or doing things —or

k) feeling agitated and unable to sit still for very long

l) feelings of worthlessness or inappropriate guilt

m) a tendency to withdraw from people, including family (often because it takes too much to go out and be with friends and have to pretend like having fun or else be a drag)

n) markedly diminished interest in things that used to be fun and difficulty taking pleasure in much of anything

o) and sometimes recurring thoughts of death as a release from the present unpleasant feelings, sometimes to the point of thinking about suicide.

If your adolescent has five or more of the above symptoms, there is a good chance that he/she is depressed, especially if they are interfering in any significant way in school, social or family functioning.

Treatment: What does one need to do to take care of this kind of problem? Since there are chemical changes that have occurred in the brain that are usually **not** permanent, it is often helpful to treat an individual with antidepressant medications. This means getting the individual to a physician for evaluation and treatment. Since general medical doctors tend to not be as experienced in these medications as psychiatrists, a referral might be in order.

There are other less pronounced depressions which may be long-standing, but not as severe. These may be sometimes approached and treated with talking therapies or counseling.

A word about Prozac and other similar medicines: Prozac has become a household word, much like Valium did in a different decade. Prozac has led the way for the development of a newer group of medicines that has made the treatment of depression much easier, because they are easier to tolerate, and thus easier to use in being treated. There are side effects, but unlike many of the previously used anti-depressants, they are much less troublesome in day to day living. Prozac has gotten a lot of press, both good and bad, but most of the bad press appears to be unwarranted, as long as the doctors prescribing the medicine follow along closely at first as they should, to make sure that any side effects which may occur are not too troublesome.

The way these medicines tend to work is to allow the natural chemicals of the brain to operate more efficiently. They do not falsely stimulate the nerves of the brain, but allow the chemicals that send messages between the cells of the brain to hang around long enough to do their work, and they also signal the cells to make more of these chemical messengers over time. They tend to be much safer than some of the older antidepressants which could kill a person in overdose, whereas Prozac and its cousins, by themselves, would cause death–(in the words of one of my colleagues) "only if the pile of pills under which they are lying is suffocating them" or if they are combined with other drugs. The cousins of Prozac are getting more numerous by the month, and each is a little different, so a doctor who is familiar with these various medicines should be consulted about their use.

Recently a lot of concern has been raised about using antidepressants in children. The fear that they may be causing suicidal feelings has arisen. I think back to when I was a young resident many years ago. Even at that time, we were warned that some individuals who are depressed may want to suicide, but do not have the energy to do so. When started on antidepressants, they may begin to get more energy before their mood improves, and when they have more energy, they may use it to try to end their lives. We were warned to carefully watch those individuals for suicidal behavior and we try to follow them quite closely in the initial stages of treatment.

Another issue to which psychiatrists have been paying more attention is the fact that antidepressants may aggravate an individual who has bipolar depression into a more agitated state, so we are more on the alert to watch for any signs of that disorder as well. One must be aware that suicide is a significant killer of youth, next to accidental death. Depression is very serious in youth, who sometimes tend to be impulse driven. Without antidepressant medicines, my personal view is that the success rates for suicidal behavior would be much higher. One should, however follow closely the directions of the prescribing physician about getting in touch if symptoms of increased agitation, increasing change in mood, thoughts about suicide, or increasing sense of hopelessness should occur.

Obsessive-Compulsive Disorder: This is an illness which is often distressing both to the individual, as well as family and others close to the afflicted individual. It consists of repetitive thoughts, ideas impulses or images of an intrusive nature, that are unwanted and may seem silly, uncomfortable or awful, and the affected individual often feels the need to do something, usually in an excessive way, to make himself comfortable about those thoughts. The thoughts may be excessive worry about dirt or germs, or may be fears about acting aggressively when one doesn't want to. They may be fears of losing something important or a need to repeatedly check something (like the stove, the door and window locks, the alarm clock) to make sure it is done properly, with the fear that something bad will happen if the checking is not carried out. As a result the individual will oftentimes wash repeatedly and excessively, take numerous showers, go through special rituals in washing clothes, dishes or other items, or avoid touching or coming into contact with objects or people. He/she may check things over and over to make sure things are done properly. Situations may be avoided where there is a worry that people will be hurt by aggressive words or behavior. Sometimes people save worthless things because of fear of safely throwing them away. People so afflicted also frequently establish rituals of behaviors that are done repeatedly and to excess, or thoughts that have to be repeated over and over in order to feel comfortable in certain situations. Repetitious counting of objects, either aloud or more commonly to oneself, is not uncommon.

Howard Hughes was clearly an individual afflicted with OCD. He became a recluse, avoiding people, fearful of germs, afraid of his food, yet he was one of the wealthiest men in the country until he died alone in his room in Nevada. Boswell recounts unusual rituals performed by Samuel Johnson in his famous biography of Johnson, implicating OCD. Many people suffer silently for months and years with the symptoms of OCD, fearing that it is "crazy" behavior, or that people will ridicule them. Many do not know what is happening to them, yet know that the thoughts and behaviors are irrational, and still feel compelled to do them, without realizing that there are treatments that are effective in alleviating or even curing them.

Treatment of OCD is effectively accomplished by using one or both of two methods. The first is to use medication. The second is to use an approach that requires structuring behavior in such a manner as to reduce the anxiety associated with the obsessive thoughts.

It has been found that the neurotransmitter serotonin (one of the chemicals used by the brain to send messages back and forth between cells in the brain) has a very reduced activity in certain areas of the brain that results in OCD. One of the ways to increase the effect of serotonin is to use a medicine that allows the serotonin naturally produced by the brain to stay around longer and to collect at the proper places so that the body's own natural substances can work more effectively. Medicines that have been found to accomplish this include Anafranil, Prozac and Luvox, but other medicines of a similar nature to Prozac have also been successfully used by some physicians, including Paxil and Zoloft. These medicines tend to be very effective for many people in the reduction of their anxiety and rituals, but while effective, are only so as long as the medicines are in place. When people stop using them, the positive effects may wear off, and the symptoms may return.

Another effective way to alleviate symptoms of OCD is an approach developed by psychologists and called a cognitive-behavioral approach. The idea is that cognition or thinking can aid the behavioral treatment. It uses two techniques in combination, **exposure** and **response prevention**, and what it does is to teach through a very structured program, by exposing the individual to the troublesome thoughts and then preventing any ritualistic response to the thoughts that were previously used to reduce anxiety. Eventually the anxiety is reduced or eliminated. Sounds simple, but it requires a certain amount of finesse by the therapist and usually meets with some resistance by the afflicted individual (and sometimes the family), because it tends to be quite uncomfortable, at least at first in the early stages of treatment.

Often family participation is important in the treatment process, because families get so caught up in the symptoms and feel sorry for the afflicted person, wanting to reduce his/her pain. It is very important in this treatment process that the family not enable the person afflicted to revert to the rituals, but help prevent the responses previously used.

More often than not, the most effective and efficient means of coping with and eliminating OCD symptoms is a combination of the above two means of treatment.

Impulse-control Disorders: Many professionals place these disorders on a continuum with OCD. They include such problems as kleptomania or pathological stealing, pyromania or the impulse to set fires, pathological gambling, explosive behavior, and trichotillomania or compulsive hair pulling, and the eating disorders. Of these, the problems seen most frequently among teens would be the explosive behavior, the hair pulling, and the eating disorders.

Treatment: The explosiveness may be softened by medication of various kinds, but in addition it is often useful to use a highly structured anger management program to teach alternatives to the explosive behavior. It adds the teaching tools the person needs to maintain a reasonable control over his/her life.

The hairpulling also sometimes responds to medications used to treat OCD, but as we have seen with many of the other treatment situations, a combination of medication and counseling or behavioral therapies is most beneficial.

Eating Disorders: Our modern culture with all of its media and press tends to accentuate the so-called physical ideal in our society. If we look in any magazine at the advertisements, for just about any product from soap to clothes to automobiles, we see the emphasis on physical attributes. Women depicted in such advertisements are usually thin, attractive and even tend to emphasize their need for a man in their lives and careers. Because adolescents are so involved in trying to sort out their own personal identities, and because they are so aware of their comparative standing with their peers, there is a great emphasis on physical appearance, attractiveness, and particularly body size. In young women, this emphasis often translates to a focus on weight, and a considerable number of young women have focused on weight to the point of being obsessed with it. Unfortunately this obsession in some has led to eating disorders that take the form of: 1) anorexia nervosa and 2) bulimia or 3) a combination of both. The hallmark of these disorders is a distorted body image and perception of being overweight beyond common sense. They often become obsessive-compulsive in their nature.

Anorexia: This is a condition in which people (most often young women) literally starve themselves, to the point of illness and even death. They frequently take on a "death camp appearance" with extreme weight loss. In extreme stages their appearance is frightful, but their own perception of themselves is not that of others. They have an extremely distorted self-image and tend to see any little amount of loose skin on their abdomen as "fat"; they often still view themselves as overweight even though experts and charts would decry the error. They often begin to experience difficulty in their thinking process because of lack of nutrition getting to their brains. They easily get cold because of the lack of insulating body fat. They begin to develop fine hair over their body as a physiological response of their bodies to cold. Often their food issues begin as a means of establishing control in their lives in a way that they are in charge, whereas they may see themselves as not able to exert that control in any other way in other areas of their lives.

Treatment: is often complicated, sometimes involving hospitalization, family therapy, individual psychotherapy, behavior modification, and sometimes medical intervention. However, early intervention may preclude many of the more complicating features of this illness. Some anorexics started out overweight, went on diets, but have become so obsessed with fat that they have shifted into an eating disorder mentality. As is often the case with anorexia and with other disorders, what starts out being one thing turns into something else.

Bulimia: Another means of controlling weight that has been adopted by some is bulimia. There is the same emphasis on body image and need for weight control, but rather than deal with starvation or hunger, many young women have found that they can eat significant amounts and then vomit. Indeed, some women get into the habit of bingeing first on food and then vomiting. It often becomes such a part of their lives that planning has to be extensive just to go on an outing, because it has to be accessible to bathrooms or suitable places to vomit discretely. Significant medical problems also arise out of this eating disorder, though not necessarily as immediately life-threatening as anorexia. However problems can occur which will surface down the road as with Karen Carpenter, who died of complications of bulimia after she had stopped the bulimic behavior. Significant blood chemistry problems can occur, damage to organs (e.g., the heart) can occur, and even the enamel can be etched off the teeth by the action of stomach acid.

Treatment: of bulimia is often as complicated as that of anorexia, and often requires a combination of medical and behavioral interventions.

Anxiety and Post-traumatic Stress Disorder: There are many forms of anxiety. Some are actually biochemical in nature; some are stress or situationally related. I will talk first about the most common kinds of anxiety, then talk about biochemically-induced anxiety, and then PTSD and phobias.

Probably the most common form that anxiety takes is what we professionals call an **Adjustment Disorder with Anxious mood**. What this means is that a situation is such that it causes an ongoing form of anxiety, usually of a moderate to mild degree, but sometimes severe. This may be anything from an upcoming major exam to a threat against one's life to concern over a medical condition.

Treatment: These forms can often be dealt with by reassurance, counseling, and support.

Generalized Anxiety Disorder is an excessive anxiety or worry that occurs more days than not for a period of time greater than 6 months, about a number of events or activities. The individual finds it difficult to control the worry. It is accompanied by:

> 1) restlessness or feeling keyed up or on edge,
> 2) being easily fatigued,
> 3) difficulty concentrating,
> 4) irritability,
> 5) muscle tension,
> 6) sleep disturbance.

Treatment: This type of anxiety may require the use of medication, but often can be alleviated by varying types of counseling or psychotherapy, partly depending on the degree of distress and impairment in one's life. Sometimes well-structured and guided forms of intervention are very useful (behavioral therapy). Sometimes examining the underlying causes of the anxiety helps.

Panic Disorder is a form of anxiety which is probably biochemical in nature, though the exact nature of the chemicals is not known. It takes the form of a sudden sense of panic, often "out of the blue". It consists of "a discrete period of intense fear or discomfort, in which four (or more) of the following symptoms developed abruptly and reached a peak within 10 minutes."

> 1) Palpitations, accelerated heart rate, or pounding heart,
> 2) Sweating,
> 3) Trembling or shaking,
> 4) Shortness of breath or sensation of smothering,
> 5) Feeling of choking,
> 6) Chest pain or discomfort,
> 7) Nausea or abdominal distress,
> 8) Feeling dizzy, lightheaded, faint or unsteady,
> 9) Feelings of unreality or being detached from oneself,
> 10) Fear of losing control or going crazy,
> 11) Fear of dying,
> 12) Numbness or tingling,
> 13) Chills or hot flushes.

Sometimes accompanying this sense of panic, is a special sensitivity to the feelings one experiences, which, in turn, makes any little reminder of those feelings to begin to feel as though the panic may again be returning. This leads to what we might call anticipatory anxiety, different from Panic Disorder, but which if left unabated, could lead to another full-blown panic episode. In other words, it is anxiety about having a panic episode, which can actually sometimes build into a panic attack if not calmed down. Some people who do not get their panic under control will become fearful of going into busy or public places. They fear the possibility of having a panic episode in such a place, because of the embarrassment or feeling out of control. They begin to avoid public places like school, church, restaurants, stores, theaters, etc. They become what is called "agoraphobic" or afraid of crowds or groups. Very often people who suffer from this disorder are reluctant to discuss it with others. They feel they are crazy, or that other people will think them weird or strange.

Treatment: There are very effective treatments for these problems. Again, both medication and behavioral techniques are useful, and often a combination of the two. Some people try to self-medicate. I have seen people get into real difficulty with alcohol over panic problems. Psychiatrists tend to be very aware of this disorder, so seeking help from such a specialist is advisable.

Social Anxiety is another form of anxiety that is sometimes mistaken as extreme shyness. This form of anxiety makes it difficult for individuals to function in group settings. They are afraid to speak in class and often fear being called on. They tend to avoid social situations and tend to isolate themselves.

Treatment: As with OCD and sometimes Panic Disorder, the combination of medication and cognitive-behavioral therapy tends to be most helpful.

Phobia is another name for an unreasonable excessive and persistent fear that is triggered by the presence or anticipation of the particular feared object or situation (flying, blood, snakes, heights, injections). Causes of phobias may vary, but the fear may long ago have distanced itself from the original cause, so that it may no longer be relevant.

Treatment: The most effective treatment for phobias is generally a treatment program that systematically exposes the person to be treated, to a gradually increasing proximity to the feared object, for gradually increasing periods of time. Many psychologists are well-trained in these techniques, as are some other clinicians such as psychiatrists, social workers, and counselors.

Post-traumatic Stress Disorder is a form of anxiety that is the direct result of a frightening situation. The event could be life-threatening or could threaten serious injury to the individual or others, and the event is experienced with intense fear or helplessness. The event is followed by intrusive recollections, recurrent distressing dreams, and/or acting or feeling as if the event were recurring (a sense of reliving the experience). Intense distress may occur when exposed to cues that resemble some part of the event, and this may be accompanied by physical bodily reactions to these feelings (excessive sweating, urge to urinate, defecate or vomit, rapid breathing). There tends to be an avoidance of things that remind one of the trauma and a general numbing of responsiveness in general, and there is a heightened arousal as if preparing for fight or flight (difficulty falling or staying asleep, irritability, difficulty concentrating, exaggerated startle response, a sense of being overly vigilant). Examples of the kind of event that might cause such distress are: experiencing an auto accident, being caught in a fire, being cornered and threatened by a gang, being raped.

Treatment: Combinations of psychotherapy and cognitive-behavioral treatments are again probably the most effective, but require the skill of a trained professional.

Other mental and emotional disorders: There are other forms of mental disorder which do not occur as often, perhaps, as the ones mentioned already, but which are of major significance when they do occur. These include schizophrenia, bipolar (manic-depressive) disorder, Tourette's Disorder, Dissociative Disorders, and Developmental Disorders (including Autism), and then there are the Personality Disorders which may be more common than we think, but for particular reasons are not always diagnosed.

Schizophrenia: The meaning of this word is "split personality" which does not mean that the person has different personalities that split off and become separate, but rather that the mind splits off from the emotions. It is a very confusing disorder, both for the person who suffers from it as well as the people who try to make sense of it. It falls in the category of mental illness called psychosis. In other words, the afflicted individual has great difficulty sorting out what is real and what is not. Thus we see a wide spectrum of symptoms. There may be hallucinations, whereby a person sees or hears things that are actually coming from within his own thoughts, but which he perceives as coming from outside himself. Sometimes there is the sense that he/she can read other people's thoughts, or that others can read his/hers. There may be the idea that special messages are being broadcast to him via the TV or radio or by other means. Sometimes there is just a gradual deterioration of thinking processes as the individual becomes more and more engrossed with his own personal world. A person may develop a very personalized world revolving around himself that allows him to begin thinking that he is someone other than who he is, or that others are not who they say they are.

182

The beginnings of this disorder are very distressing. The afflicted individual is trying to make sense of a series of confusing and conflicting feelings and thoughts. Imagine, for example, that someone whom you have known all your life has been replaced by someone whom you do not know and yet looks very much like the person he says he is. Yet, for some reason, you know he is not that person. Or, imagine beginning to hear voices telling you that you should harm yourself or do things that you know that you should not. Or imagine that you have been given a special duty to perform a task that will have great significance to the world, but other people will not accept this as true. Or again, imagine that some conspiracy is taking place that will harm you, and you don't exactly know how, except that you are sure that it is going on, and you must keep alert to try to figure it out, and who is trying to hurt you. Sometimes things are not even this clear. It is just a jumble of confusing thoughts and feelings.

Treatment: For many years there was no effective treatment for schizophrenia, and people were placed in large hospitals or tolerated as eccentrics. In the 1950's a new group of medicines was discovered that had numerous side effects, but also helped reverse many of the incapacitating symptoms of schizophrenia. These medicines were called phenothiazines and included Thorazine, Stelazine and Mellaril. Over the years many other kinds of medicine were developed which have been helpful in reducing the impact of this illness on the individuals and their families. Some of these can be given in long-acting form such as injections that are administered once a month or so. They include Haldol and Prolixin, and more recently other medicines that have been very effective have been Clozaril and Risperdal. These medicines are administered under the direction of a psychiatrist trained in their use. The important thing about these medicines is that they be taken regularly as prescribed. Where people get into trouble with them is when they stop taking them.

There are some important side effects to these medicines that should be known about. These include side effects that are immediate, and those that are late in arrival ("tardive"). The immediate side effects are distressing, but not often major in their potential for harm. They can usually be easily interrupted.

The "tardive" problems, on the other hand, are movement disorders which may be irreversible if not caught early, so it is important to know about them and to get information from the doctor about them. Metabolic changes also occur in many of these medications.

People who suffer from schizophrenia also often need to be taught to do things in a way that is socially acceptable, so oftentimes other programs that help them to be involved appropriately with others can be very helpful. Sometimes sheltered workshops can help them to learn work skills in a setting that can also teach them the social skills to be able to work around other people. Frequently such programs are able to be accessed through the local mental health clinics.

Bipolar Disorder: This is an illness that is also known as **Manic-depressive Disorder**. It is an illness that is essentially a disorder of mood, rather than a thought disorder like schizophrenia, but it can result in distortions of reality. It is called bipolar, because it has two swings of mood, high and low. The low is the depression; the high is the manic behavior. There is a continuum of severity of this disorder. Some people swing from a mild somewhat euphoric state which may feel very productive, to a moody, morose feeling where very little can seem to get done. This milder state is sometimes referred to as cyclothymia. However some people shift from a very pressured state of activity, where they sleep very little, talk very rapidly, their thoughts race, and they feel like they can do just about anything, then tend to get overextended in various projects. Then they go to a very depressed state of feeling overwhelmed, unable to get up and out to do their work, fearful, crying, exhausted, and sometimes suicidal. The illness is sometimes characterized by the manic episodes, which often feel good to the patient, and can even result in grandiose delusions of excessive ability or power. At other times they are predominantly of a depressive character. They can be very disruptive to everyday life.

Treatment: There are a number of treatments, partly depending on the rapidity of the cycling, the frequency of attacks, and response to various medications. Since this is an organic illness,

184

and like schizophrenia, does tend to run in families, the most helpful treatments tend to be medicines. The episodes of mania most often precede the depressive attacks, and the manic state is often precipitated or aggravated by not getting enough sleep and rest, by overworking, and by not taking the time to rest, so one of the interventions is to encourage the person to take breaks, get rest and sleep. The idea of "kindling" is important. If one wants to start a fire, one does not light a match and hold it to a log. Instead, one lights some paper, then small twigs and kindling; then when the blaze is sufficient, one puts the log on the fire. The same notion applies to bipolar disorder, but in this case, we try to prevent the kindling from catching by getting enough rest and breaks.

In regard to medicine, the most effective one found so far seems to be a form of salt called **lithium carbonate**. It is a very simple compound made up of carbon and oxygen and a very light metal called lithium. The common salt on our tables is sodium chloride. Lithium is in the same family as sodium. Sodium bicarbonate is common baking soda. Lithium has to be prescribed by a doctor. It also has to be carefully monitored, but it can tend to be very effective in controlling the bipolar illness. If people do not tolerate lithium well for one reason or another, there are some other medicines used to help control the symptoms, and these are medicines used to treat seizures. They are carbamazepine or Tegretol, valproic acid or Depakote, clonazepam or Klonopin, Trileptal and Lamictal. Some of these anticonvulsant mood stabilizers are more effective in the rapid cycling and mixed state (both depressed and agitated at the same time) types of bipolar disorder.

One should keep in mind that this illness can be very disruptive, and should be treated. People in manic states can be very amusing and entertaining, and appear to be having a great time, but they will wear others out around them in short order, and eventually they wear themselves out as well. Their mania tends to make them feel as though they are productive, but if one looks at what gets done, it is very little, and once the depression hits, forget productivity. Suicide is a serious threat in bipolar disorder.

Tourette's Disorder: Originally named after the French doctor who described it, Gilles de la Tourette, this malady was almost considered an oddity. The people who suffered from it were found to utter profanities in public places, to make unusual and stereotyped movements, and generally to act very strangely in public in a way that was not socially acceptable. Now we see this disorder as a disorder of movement which is neurological in nature, though we do not know exactly how it comes about. Yet the psychological ramifications are also very prominent, because people who suffer from it continue to have the urge to do the things that were considered so socially unacceptable before. The disorder is primarily one of **tics**, but there is also a strong component of obsessive-compulsive features as well. The tics are jerking movements of the head, grimacing movements of the face, and vocal utterances, sometime of a gutteral nature, sometimes muttering profanities. There can also be respiratory tics, having to do with unusual breathing patterns. The tics occur many times a day, often in bouts, and can occur at night during sleep. People who suffered from this disorder in the past often ended up living very isolated lives, because they could not easily function in society with the social inappropriateness of their tics.

Treatment: There are a number of medicines which have been tried with Tourette's, some with good success. Some have been helpful in reducing or eliminating the tics. Some of the more complex tics, involving a combination of tics and obsessive-compulsive features, can also be helped with medicines. It is not infrequent that ADHD coincides with Tourette's, and so Ritalin and Clonidine are also sometimes used in some combination with other medicines. Treatment usually takes the art of an experienced clinician.

Developmental Disorders: This category includes many kinds of difficulties that children are born with. They include mental retardation, learning disorders such as dyslexia, and **pervasive developmental disorders** including autism and Asperger's disorder. I include this group in this chapter mainly to point out that though autism may resemble schizophrenia in some instances, it is not the same. Schizophrenia usually develops in adolescence or early adulthood, sometimes in childhood, but autism is present usually from birth. Though both may have similar characteristics to some extent later in life, the autistic child, and later adolescent, is usually distant, difficult to relate to and lacking in social and emotional response from a very early age. As with schizophrenia, the autistic child can be bright, but achievement is limited because of the difficulty in connecting with other people. The autistic child tends to fail to develop peer relationships appropriate to his/her age group; autistic children tend to lack reciprocal relationships when approached with emotional content from others. They don't spontaneously seek to share interests or enjoyment with others, and they tend to be very impaired in using the usual nonverbal behaviors that we all use to help us communicate and interact socially, such as facial expressions, eye contact, body postures and gestures.

Autistic youngsters can learn to accommodate in a limited fashion in some instances, and can sometimes learn to function in society. There is a wide variation in ability in autistic individuals. Among one of my patients was a young man who was about to graduate successfully from college.

Treatment: There are no presently known medicines that will counteract the developmental gaps in autism. What we know to do, is to make sure that they are caught as early as possible, and taught such things as language, reasonable social expectations, and to refrain from aggressive behavior. Teaching and training seem to be our best means of impacting education and socialization in this mysterious ailment.

Dissociative Disorders: This is a group of disorders that is not very common in adolescents, though many of them would like to have this kind of an excuse for getting into trouble. The predominant symptom is a disruption in conscious awareness of the environment or memory. It may take the form of amnesia for an event, waking up somewhere, for example, and not knowing how one got there. This is to be differentiated from an alcoholic or drug blackout. It may take the form of "depersonalization", a persistent or recurring feeling of detachment from one's own mental processes, like watching oneself in a dream. This kind of feeling is not all that uncommon in teens, but if persistent, may become a problem. The most pronounced dissociative problem is what is now termed Dissociative Identity Disorder and was formerly referred to as Multiple Personality Disorder. It occurs in people who have been seriously abused in their past and have developed the dissociative mechanism to escape or better cope with the abuse. In these people, the different dissociative events actually take on personalities for the handling of that event, and other similar events which may occur over the passage of time. The greatest problem comes with the lack of communication between the different "alters" (awareness states) and the confusion and social and legal difficulties caused as a result.

Treatment: The main kind of treatment for these problems is not medicine, but rather psychotherapy by someone skilled in their treatment. A person who suffers from dissociative disorders, though serious, is not considered psychotic, though sometimes the degree of impairment sometimes approaches psychotic proportions in its severity. It is very important to diagnose these conditions accurately. One does not want to label a condition which tends to be very dramatic in its appearance, and potentially could be expanded on by a histrionic individual. Some professionals, for example, think that Multiple Personality Disorder is "iatrogenic" (caused by the treater of the disease). It certainly can be accentuated or aggravated by the therapist if not treated with great care.

Personality Disorders: As mentioned above, these disorders are not disorders of thinking, but rather maladaptive habit patterns of living. They are typified by the turmoil caused around them which the individual does not seem as bothered by as those who impinge on that person's life. When you see other people scurrying around to try to resolve the problems which have arisen in the person's life, and seem to be more concerned and actively involved in resolving the problems than the individual himself, consider that you may be dealing with someone with a personality disorder. There are a number of personality disorders, but I will mention only a few which are more commonly encountered in adolescence. They are:

Antisocial: This personality disorder is actually not to be diagnosed prior to age 18. Also, a history of **conduct disorder** must be present since before age 15. Conduct disorder (a childhood disorder) is a repetitive pattern of behavior in which the basic rights of others or other significant social norms are persistently violated. It usually involves lying, stealing, destruction of property and aggression to people and/or animals.

The pervasive pattern of the antisocial personality is one of disregard for and violation of the rights of others. These individuals tend to be deceitful, impulsive, irritable and aggressive, reckless with disregard for the safety of themselves or others, irresponsible, reluctant to follow social norms or rules, and having little respect for the feelings of others, thus having little or no remorse for the ramifications of their behavior on others. They frequently end up in trouble with the law, and many end up spending some time in prison. The more "successful" ones tend to be smooth-talking people who manipulate others to their own benefit.

Narcissistic: These individuals have a great need for admiration, and they have an exaggerated sense of self-importance. They tend to lack empathy for others and to have a preoccupation with fantasies of their own brilliance, beauty, power and success. They consider themselves unique and special and have a strong sense of "entitlement" or expectation that they should be treated according to this specialness. They tend to lack empathy for others, to be envious of the successes of others, and to take advantage of others for their own gain. They are generally arrogant and demand excessive admiration.

Histrionic: These people tend to be excessively emotional with strong attention-seeking behavior. They want to be the center of attention, and their interactions with others are often inappropriately sexually seductive or provocative. They frequently use their physical appearance to draw attention to themselves and tend to be overly dramatic or even theatrical with exaggerated expressions of emotion. They are easily suggestible and influenced by others, but see their relationships with others (which are often shallow) as being more substantial than they really are. They tend to speak in a way that is affected, but nonspecific and lacking details.

Borderline: This is one of the more severe personality disorders. These people were originally seen as existing on the border between psychotic and neurotic. Indeed, some of the more severe cases do decompensate into brief periods of psychosis, particularly when under stress or when there is a lack of structure or direction in their lives. When there is a good deal of structure in their lives, they tend to look OK, but when the structure is gone, they tend to look confused or disorganized, and often unable to track well. They tend to have a strong fear of abandonment, yet when people get too close, there is a strong fear and aversion to being engulfed and taken over by others. There is a frequent use of a defense called "splitting", which means that things are all or none, black or white, either this or the opposite. Thus the borderline either hates a person or thinks that person is great. Parents are either stupid and mean or wonderful and generous. This splitting can shift very rapidly, so that a borderline child can be angry and swearing at parents one moment and asking for a ride to the shopping center the next, as though nothing had ever happened. Relationships tend to be intense but unstable and marked by anger or depression, while on the surface these individuals tend to look superficially stable. They tend to be impulsive (with sex, spending money, substance abuse, or driving recklessly) and they tend to be very intense and reactive in their mood. There are often suicidal gestures or attempts and self mutilating behavior, and when asked, they will often volunteer ongoing feelings of emptiness.

Treatment: Because these habit patterns of living are what we call "ego-syntonic" or, in other words, OK or comfortable, as far as the afflicted individual is concerned, they are more difficult to treat than if the individual felt that they were uncomfortable. Unless the discomfort of people around these individuals is turned back onto the individuals themselves, they are very difficult to get to. Most often, the most effective means of treatment starts with confrontation, not necessarily nose-to-nose confrontation, but some means of letting them know that others will not let them pursue behaviors that cause these other people discomfort. Containment of these behaviors will often cause anger at first, but as the containment continues, depression. As the depression continues, the individual then becomes available for emotional access, as long as the containment continues and the individual is not allowed to escape into behaviors that give them emotional release (i.e., the old maladaptive behaviors).

These disorders are very difficult to treat and require a therapist who has had experience in dealing with many different types of disorders, as well as having some significant life experience, and someone who can work with other family members who have to contend with the behaviors.

Teen Suicide: Suicide ranks third as the leading cause of death among young people (behind accidents and homicide). For people between age 15 and 19, it is the second leading cause of death. There are 14 suicides for every 100,000 adolescents in the U.S. each year, and about 14 people between the ages of 15 and 24 die every day in this country by suicide. Over the past 35 years, the suicide rate has tripled and rates between the ages of 10 and 14 have increased 120% since 1980. Firearms are the most commonly used method among young people, and they account for 2 of every 3 completed suicides. While the typical profile of an attempt at suicide is that of a female who ingests pills, the typical completer of suicide is the male who uses a firearm. Research has shown that access to or the availability of firearms is a significant factor in the increase of youth suicide. Attempts at suicide are reported by 14% of all adolescents. A prior suicide attempt is an important risk factor for an eventual completion. Up to 60% of high school students report having suicidal ideation.

Suicide risk factors include (but are not limited to):

1) Presence of a psychiatric disorder (e.g., depression, manic-depression, personality disorder, conduct disorder).

2) Substance abuse or dependency.

3) Expressions or communications of thoughts of suicide, death, dying or the afterlife (in the context of boredom, sadness, or negative feeling).

4) Poor control over behavior or significant change in behavior.

5) Impulsive or aggressive behavior or frequent expressions of rage.

6) Previous exposure to their own or others' suicidality.

7) Recent severe stressors.

8) Family losses or instability; significant problems in parental relationships.

9) Difficulties in dealing with sexual orientation; unplanned pregnancy.

10) History of running away or incarceration.

Suicide can be a very contagious problem. In the 1800's, there was a book written by Goethe, the famous German author of <u>Faust</u>, which resulted in an epidemic of suicides among young men. It was <u>The Sorrows of Young Werther</u>, and told of a young man who was despondent over unrequited love. Suicide today may also be contagious. There is definitely a susceptibility to imitative suicide, as has been seen in the death of Curt Kolbein. There is also glamorization (for the attention or recognition) as an element, and sometimes a sense of glorification or reverence is involved. All too often there is a lack of sense of mortality among youth. In my experience, there is often an underlying concept of a different level of consciousness that will ensue after death, and a continuing on in a different manner of being.

When observing signs that a person is depressed, or may be thinking about suicide—offer to listen and to help where you can. Go ahead and ask, and take any talk about or hint of suicide seriously. Don't be afraid to follow your suspicions. Better to do so than to be sorry later. Avoid judgment or moralizing, and do what you can to get the person to a professional who knows how to deal with this kind of issue. Don't be afraid to ask direct questions about whether the person has thought of killing themselves or how they planned to do so—or what impact they think it would have on others. Also, whether there would be anything that would change how they feel, or if they would consider a trial at seeing someone who might be able to help them.

How does someone get help for kids with various kinds of problems? There are a number of ways to seek help for your troubled teenager. The first thing one has to decide is what type of professional help is needed. This depends partly on where the trouble is showing up. If at school, sometimes the school counselor can be of help in making a referral. If it appears medical, sometimes the pediatrician or family doctor can either prescribe or refer to another qualified mental health person, a psychologist, psychiatrist, counselor or social worker. In looking back over this chapter, there are a variety of illnesses that are best referred to a medical person, others that are very well dealt with by other mental health professionals. Sometimes the best referral information comes from other people who have had success with a particular professional person. Sometimes it comes from a referral organization or agency in your area. The local medical society is often a great resource for psychiatrists and particularly child and adolescent psychiatrists in your area. The local psychological association is likewise a resource for psychologists. If there is a hospital with a mental health unit in your area, the professional staff there may be able to steer you to appropriate resources.

Organizations such as The Alliance for the Mentally Ill may be able to help families with members who suffer with major psychoses. Other organizations offer information about other specific illnesses such as OCD and Tourette's Disorder. There will be an appendix to this chapter which will list various organizations, books, movies, and other resources available to give people guidance in these matters.

Pearls For Parents:

1) Don't buy the old notion that all teenagers have all kinds of problems just on the basis of their age and the stages of their lives. If kids are having troubles, check it out.

2) If you don't understand something that is happening with your child, seek advice from a professional who works in this area. Don't underestimate the distress the child may be having and the toll it may be taking on his education, peer relationships or his self-confidence. If it is nothing or is normal, let a pro tell you.

3) Be assertive as a consumer both with doctors and other providers as well as with insurance company representatives. You have a right to the service they are providing, as long as you are not rude or overly aggressive.

4) Kids don't usually know if something is wrong with them any more than you do. Be patient with them. Remember, as teenagers, their first response is often one of resistance to what you as a parent will want them to do. Even if you run your household as a democracy, there must be leaders and people in charge, and that happens to be you, so don't be bashful about asserting yourself with your kid and telling him that he will be seeing a professional. However, if you can, avoid getting into a power struggle about it. Just deal with it as if it is a given fact that is going to happen.

Appendix For Mental Health In Adolescents:

Resources (organizations, books, movies):
Most of these organizations can be found using Google.
American Academy of Child and Adolescent Psychiatry is a referral
source for board-certified child and adolescent psychiatrists.
http://www.aacap.org/
Anorexia Nervosa and Associated Disorders
Anorexia Nervosa and Related Eating Disorders
Anxiety Disorders Association of America
Association for the Advancement of Behavior Therapy
Autism Research Institute
Child & Adolescent Psychopharmacology Information Center
CH. A. D. D. Children and Adults with Attention Deficit Disorders
Depression and Related Affective Disorders Association (DRADA)

Learning Disabilities Association of America
Lithium Information Center
National Alliance for the Mentally Ill (NAMI)
National Center for Learning Disabilities
Depression and Bipolar Support Alliance
National Foundation for Depressive Illness
National Information Center for Children & Youth with Handicaps
National Institute of Mental Health
National Mental Health Association
Obsessive-Compulsive Foundation
Obsessive-Compulsive Information Center
Orton Dyslexia Society
Tourette Syndrome Association

Books:
ADHD
Out of the Fog by Kevin R. Murphy Ph.D. and Suzanne LeVert—
    Hyperion Press
Driven To Distraction by Edward M. Hallowell M.D. and John J. Ratey
    M.D. Touchstone Books—Simon and Schuster
The Hyperactive Child, Adolescent, and Adult by Paul Wender M.D. Ox-
    ford University Press, 1987

Hyperactive Children by Russell Barkley—Guilford Press—
    New York—1981
Assertive Discipline For Parents by Canter, Lee & Canter, Margaret Canter
    & Associates, Inc.
Attention Deficit Disorder and Hyperactivity by Ronald Friedman Educa-
    tional Resources, Inc.
What is Attention Deficit Disorder and How Does Medication Help? by
    Barry Garfinkel
The Misunderstood Child by Larry Silver
    McGraw Hill 1984

Autism:

Extraordinary People Understanding the Savant Syndrome by Darold
    Treffert, M.D. Ballantine Books New York 1989
An Anthropologist On Mars by Oliver Sacks p. 188 "Prodigies" Alfred A.
    Knopf Publisher New York 1995
Bipolar Disorder (Manic-Depressive): Moodswing by Ronald R. Fieve—
    Bantam Books

We Heard The Angels of Madness: How One Family Dealt With Manic
      Depression by Diane Berger—William Morrow and Co.

Eating Disorders:

The Golden Cage by Hilda Bruch MD Harvard University Press 1978
Eating Disorders by Hilda Bruch MD Basic Books, Inc. 1973
Panic Disorder: The Anxiety Disease by David Sheehan
      Bantam Books 1990

Borderline Personality Disorder:

I Hate You—-Don't Leave Me by Jerold J. Kreisman MD and Hal Straus—
      Avon Books 1991

Obsessive Compulsive Disorder:

Getting Control: Overcoming Your Obsessions and Compulsions
      by L. Baer—Boston: Little, Brown and Co. 1991
Stop Obsessing! How to Overcome Your Obsessions and Compulsions
      by Edna B. Foa New York: Bantam; 1991
Fears, Phobias and Rituals by I.M. Marks
      New York: Oxford U. Press: 1978
When Once Is Not Enough: Help for Obsessive Compulsives by G. Stele-
      tee and K. White
      Oakland, Cal: New Harbinger Publications, Inc; 1990
Obsessive Compulsive Disorder: A Guide by John H. Greist M.D.—
      Madison, WI: Dean Foundation for Health Researc and
      Education; 1993

Anxiety and Its Treatment: Help Is Available by John Greist, James Jeffer-
      son, and I.M. Marks—Washington DC: American Psychiatric Press
      - 1986:69

Depression:

The Human Season by Edward Lewis Wallant (author of The Pawnbro-
      ker) Harbrace Paperbound Library
      Harcourt Brace Jovanovich, Inc. New York 1960

Tourette's Disorder:

An Anthropologist On Mars by Oliver Sacks p.77 "A Surgeon's Life"
      Alfred A Knopf publisher 1995
Teaching The Tiger—a guide for teachers and parents of Tourette's
      kids—Hope Press General:

The Adolescent Through Fiction by Norman Kiell —International Universities Press, Inc. New York copyright 1958, paperback edition 1974.

Child Development Through Literture
edited by Elliott D. Landau, Sherrie Landau Epstein,
Ann Plaat Stone. Prentice-Hall, Inc., Englewood Cliffs, New Jersey 1972

The Abnormal Personality Through Literature edited by Alan A. Stone, M.D. and Sue Smart Stone

Prentice-Hall, Inc., Englewood Cliffs, New Jersey 1966

Insights A Selection Of Creative Literature About Children selected and edited by the Child Study Association of America Introduction and Comment by Anna W. M. Wolf 1973

Classic Movies:

Autism:

"Rain Man" (Dustin Hoffman, Tom Cruise)
"Cries From The Heart" (Patty Duke, Melissa Gilbert)

Depression:

"Ordinary People" (Timothy Hutton, Donald Sutherland, Mary Tyler Moore, Judd Hirsch)
Dissociative Disorder:
"Three Faces of Eve" (Joanne Woodword, Lee J. Cobb)
"Sybil" (Sally Field, Joanne Woodward)
Psychosis:
"The Fisher King" (Robin Williams) "Shine" (Geoffrey Rush)
"A Beautiful Mind (Russell Crowe)

Suicide:

"The Big Chill" (Tom Berenger, Glenn Close, William Hurt, Meg Tilly, Jo Beth Williams, Kevin Kline, Jeff Goldblum, Mary Kay Place)

Eating Disorders:

"For The Love of Nancy" (Jill Clayburgh)
"Kate's Secret" (Ed Asner)

Chapter 10
DRUGS AND ALCOHOL
IN ADOLESCENTS

"Miniver Cheevy, child of scorn, Grew lean while he assailed the seasons;
He wept that he was ever born, And he had reasons …
Miniver Cheevy, born too late, Scratched his head and kept on thinking;
Miniver coughed and called it fate, And kept on drinking.
—**Edwin Arlington Robinson "Miniver Cheevy"**

History And General Facts:

Alcohol has been with mankind since the earliest times, and various drug forms have been used since antiquity. Mankind has attempted from early times to use what nature has provided to aid in soothing the ills of the world. Homer described Odysseus giving the Cyclops strong wine to drug him so he could blind him while he slept. References to excesses of strong wine also occur in the Old Testament. As we look to the middle ages, use of various plant poisons was a common means of disposing of enemies. Clearly, over time, alcohol and various plant derivatives became very important in religious and social rituals and became commonplace in most cultures. Native Americans used peyote, a hallucinogen derived from cactus buttons, in their religious rituals. Jews and Christians use wine in their ceremonies and prayers. Others have used hallucinogenic mushrooms in similar fashion. Some cultures have had drugs pushed upon them for economic reasons such as the Europeans did with opium in China and white men did with alcohol to the native Americans a century ago. Some cultures have used wine because the water was not always safe to drink. Over the centuries, alcohol has had more impact on the economic condition of man than any other drug.

In our present day culture, it is not uncommon for adolescents to become indoctrinated to the notion that use, and sometimes excessive use, of alcohol and other substances, like marijuana, hallucinogenic drugs, stimulants, and opiates are not only common but an acceptable and preferable practice. Many of these drugs have become relatively easy to access, and peer and social pressure can influence many to experimentation, and sometimes to habituation and addiction. This leads to major effects on lifestyle and habits, and subsequently to changes in performance and in family life.

Some General Notions About Drugs And Alcohol:

1) Most, if not all drugs, are generally toxins or, otherwise known as **poisons** to the human system. Many drugs are toxins. The drugs used to fight cancers are toxins; many heart drugs are toxins; some antidepressants are toxins. By this we mean that used in excess, they can kill the individual who takes them, or at least significantly impair the use of bodily functions. The reason they cause the effect that they do is usually because of their effect on the functioning of the brain.

2) Drugs tend to be **very available** to teens. Marijuana, LSD, amphetamines (speed, crank), alcohol, and even cocaine can be easily obtained if a teen knows the right person, and that person may well be a kid in the hall at junior high or high school.

3) Even if your kid is a straight shooter, do not underestimate the effect of **peer pressure**. Many young people start out using by just trying something out. Those who use the stuff have to start sometime. Sometimes a kid is more vulnerable because of a social shift in the group of kids that he has been hanging out with. Sometimes another kid who is a leader will make a shift for his/her own reasons and carry along others by his/her influence.

4) How do you tell when your kid is experimenting—or maybe habituated—or even addicted to a drug? The first thing that tends to be a sign is a **change in patterns of behavior**—life style changes. For example, if a youngster who use to bathe and keep clean suddenly stops paying attention to his/her physical hygiene, stops bathing, brushing teeth, combing hair, etc.—beware, and observe other behaviors. If a child starts losing weight, skin looks not quite right with more pimples or areas where the child has been picking at it a lot, one should particularly be concerned about amphetamines. If stealing becomes a problem, things turn up missing, the child's stories don't add up, reasons for things that are new or different suddenly turning up somehow don't make much sense, then start pinning the kid down. Start tracking his/her whereabouts more closely.

Many kids will experiment with alcohol or some drugs such as marijuana, but when their life style changes significantly, they are probably more than just experimenting. Also, always remember, **you can always tell when an addict is lying, because his lips will be moving.** Also, as a general rule, kids will lie if they think it will keep them out of trouble. Just because they have always been straight with you does not mean they will not lie if cornered and fearful of the consequences.

Another sign of drug use that goes along with the idea of life style changes is when a child begins to screw up in school. Grades drop. Teachers are frustrated with a change in attitude. Interest which was there before now begins to drop. Likewise, with a child who has been actively involved in sports, who suddenly loses interest, one should be watchful and start asking questions.

If a child becomes irritable and his/her attention span becomes shortened; if the child is not tracking well all of a sudden, start investigating, and **don't buy phony or lame sounding excuses.** If unfamiliar items show up, make the kid show some legitimate receipts or documentation for what he/she says is true. If it doesn't sound right, don't be afraid to call other parents or give the teachers a call. Don't be afraid to call the school about attendance or to require the kid to bring signatures on notes from teachers. Also, don't forget that the child's doctor can easily order urine or blood tests for drug abuse.

5) What kinds of things **predispose** kids to using drugs and alcohol?

Unfortunately, many young people are so acclimatized to alcohol that it is accepted as just part of the normal life of many high school and college age youth. General acceptance among their peers makes it easy to use alcohol and to some extent marijuana. However those youngsters who are alienated from their more achieving peers often tend to find others who feel the same sense of frustration and alienation, and they gravitate toward one another. Often these are kids who don't make it academically and want to find some measure of success somewhere. They also may not make it in sports, so that avenue is also cut off for acceptance. Sometimes they will look for it in the drama department at school, in the chess club or in groups who do gaming, but many of the kids who get involved in drugs are those who find it difficult to stick it out and persist in activities, so they may not make it in that setting either. This does not mean that good athletes and students do not try or use drugs; it does mean, however, that kids who **struggle with a sense of self-esteem** are those who may be most predisposed to be affected by drugs. However, let's not forget that the **impact of** what others are doing in the **family** may also predispose kids to use. If there is an attitude in the family that alcohol is part of everyday existence, if there is no inhibition about using marijuana or other drugs by the parents or by siblings, that attitude will carry over. If violence and disregard for others is rampant, one cannot expect that such attitudes will not be learned by the way they are modeled. If abuse occurs in the family, other undesirable behaviors follow.

6) What is the **effect of drugs on performance?** Many people who are using alcohol, marijuana, LSD, amphetamines, and other substances, feel that while they are "high", they actually have enhanced performance. Nothing could be further from the truth. Alcohol has been demonstrated to decrease reflex time

and to inhibit the thinking process. Marijuana may give the feeling of being more in touch with the realities of the world, but it clearly reduces both production and ambition, and also slows reflex time. Amphetamines tend to give the impression to the user of being more alert and with it, but performance clearly is diminished under the influence of this substance. Certainly the various inhalants, which I have not yet mentioned also numb both thinking and performance and present an added danger of liver damage. In regard to hallucinogens like LSD, perhaps it is summed up best by the comment of a parent, "Why anyone would purposely make themselves schizophrenic is beyond me."

7) What is the **effect on families**? The impact of drug use by one family member cannot help but be felt by all family members. In those families where a teen gets involved in repetitive drug use, there are not only the issues of family distress, but major economic and liability factors as well. Remember that as parents of a teen, you are **legally responsible** for the kinds of trouble that that child may get into, **including fines, damages, and lawsuits**. Also remember that other children in the family tend to be negatively impacted, not only by the chaos that ensues, but by the modeling of that particular behavior and the modeling of whatever the consequences of that behavior may be on the person who is committing it. The other thing is that as the drug seeking and using behavior gets more and more out of control, the whole idea of living in that kind of chaos becomes more and more painful to everyone involved.

Classes Of Drugs:

Alcohol: (Common names include booze, hootch, suds, brew, keg, hard stuff, coolers, and many names too numerous to list).

It comes in many forms, and is primarily made by fermenting sugars, usually of some naturally occurring fruit or plant. It can be made from many sources including grapes, rice, potatoes, dandelions, various berries and fruits, and grains. It takes the forms of beer, wine, distilled liquors, sweetened liqueurs, wine coolers, mead, ale, and others too numerable to list. There are actually many kinds of alcohol, but ethyl alcohol is the form found when fructose (fruit sugar) and glucose (table sugar) are fermented. After the fermenting process has taken place, sometimes individuals then distill off the alcohol by boiling it up into copper coils and recooling it to condense into a collecting container, thus concentrating the alcohol itself in the container. This results in various forms of whiskey and brandy, depending on what the original source of sugar was. (Molasses = rum, corn = whiskey, grapes and other fruits = brandy, rye = Canadian whiskey, cactus = tequila, honey = mead, etc.) When the alcohol remains in the original juice of the fruit or berry, it remains wine. Beers are usually made from barley, but are flavored with the leaves of the hops plant. Many beers these days are produced in microbreweries, that is, they are produced in small breweries right on the premises of the various pubs and bars where they are sold.

Alcohol is a toxin or poison to the central nervous system (brain and spinal cord). It is metabolized or broken down fairly quickly in the liver, provided that organ is in good working order, but if ingested too quickly, or if the liver is hampered in its ability to break it down (as in the case, for example, of someone who has liver disease such as hepatitis or whose liver is affected by mononucleosis), the alcohol impacts further on the brain's ability to carry out its normal functions. The effects of this toxin on the brain are to decrease reaction time, resulting in slower physical response (and an increase in auto accidents while under the influence); decrease in inhibitions (a given individual normally has certain reservations about behavior, but alcohol tends to eliminate or decrease those reservations resulting in rash or poor judgment). This is particularly a problem when sexual opportunities occur.

Alcohol, like other drugs, can be **addicting**. What that means is that the body becomes acclimatized to the drug and craves it when it is not present in the quantities that the body has become used to. In addition, tolerance develops. That means that the quantity needed by the body continues to increase, so that the individual has to take in more and more to satisfy the physical

204

craving. Eventually the body craves greater quantities than the individual can possibly ingest in a given time, and withdrawal symptoms can set in even when the person continues to drink. This is what DT's are all about. Withdrawal symptoms can also occur at any time along the way once the individual is addicted. All that needs to occur is for the supply of alcohol to stop abruptly. Withdrawal symptoms include shakiness, irritability, nausea, sweating, diarrhea, visual and sensory hallucinations, seizures and even death. **DT's are delirium tremens and are a severe form of alcohol withdrawal** which usually takes the form of severe agitation, hallucinations, and seizures. They usually occur in later stages of alcoholism but are very serious and can be fatal. Anyone in severe withdrawal from alcohol should be under a physician's care.

Alcohol poisoning can occur when a large amount of alcohol is consumed quickly and the individual is overcome by the toxin, passes out, and respiration may be suppressed, or vomiting may occur and the individual may aspirate (breathe in the vomit) and choke. Either of these can lead to death.

Signs of alcohol use include: smelling of alcohol, loss of inhibitions and worries, slowed reactions, slurred speech, disorientation, staggering, poor judgment, and loss of control over behavior, including aggression or violence or any significant change of personality.

Long term use can result in addiction or psychological dependence, depression, personality change, or physical damage to heart, liver and other organs or injury secondary to a variety of accidents which can occur.

Marijuana: (common names include pot, grass, weed, roach, bud, dope, joint, reefer, Acapulco Gold, Mexican, Columbian, sens, sinsemilla, Mary Jane, Mary, and again, many other names too numerous to list).

Marijuana is a form of cannabis, a plant family which includes hemp and hashish. At one time during World War II the U.S. government planted marijuana along the roadways in Iowa and other midwest states in case our hemp supplies were cut off by the war. Hemp is used to make rope, and at the time marijuana use in the States was not a significant problem. Marijuana is easily grown and thus is not easily eradicated.

People who use cannabis talk about being "stoned" or high. It generally tends to give the user a sense of calm and sometimes a sense of being able to have greater insights into the world. It does decrease inhibitions and slow reaction time as does alcohol. It also tends to result in poor concentration, loss of ambition and motivation, some loss of memory, and sometimes, disorientation. Physically it tends to weaken immune systems and gives a higher risk of lung cancer because it is generally smoked. It can also negatively affect the reproductive system.

Signs of use include red or bloodshot eyes, glassy eyes, increased appetite (the munchies), interference with perception of time, giddy response or silly, happy and talkative behavior, or sometimes quiet, withdrawn, confused or frightened behavior. Speech is sometimes affected.

Marijuana comes in **different forms**: dried leaves and buds, dark brown cubes of pressed resin (hash), distilled oil of the resin (hash oil), cooked into brownies. It can be eaten as brownies, smoked as a home-made cigarette, or smoked in a bong (a water bottle with a pipe attached to draw the smoke through the water). With the advent of legalization in some states, there is more production of "edibles" or candy-like forms of cannabis of varying strengths.

Amphetamines: Often called "Poor man's cocaine", these drugs are stimulants. They include Benzedrine, Dexedrine (dextroamphetamine) and Adderall (amphetamine) and are often prescription drugs which used to be used widely as appetite suppressants for weight loss, or treatment for Attention Deficit Hyperactivity Disorder. (Ritalin, another stimulant for treating ADHD may also be abused.) They come in the form of pills, and thus are ingested or "dropped". They also come in the form of **methamphetamine**, which is an illegal, potent, fast acting amphetamine which comes in the form of powder, clear liquid or tablets. It is used by inhaling, smoking, swallowing or injecting. Though amphetamines can legitimately be used in the treatment of Attention Deficit Disorder, they are also prone to be abused.

Pocket mirrors and razor blades are sometimes used for preparing "lines" of meth to be snorted or inhaled as with cocaine.

Common names for amphetamines are: uppers, bennies, crosstops, black beauties, dexies, beans, and pep pills. Other names which more frequently apply to methamphetamine include crank, speed, crystal, meth, rose, and water.

Teens tend to obtain some amphetamines by stealing them from their parents' medicine cabinet, or from burglaries. However meth is often very available these days on the streets. Meth production tends to create a foul, rancid odor sometimes described as smelling like cat urine.

Signs of use include: bad breath, bright shiny eyes, dilated (large) pupils, sweating, dry mouth and lips, difficulty sleeping, loss of appetite, increased pulse rate and blood pressure, and sometimes mental confusion. They may be overactive, talkative, and capable of irrational behavior. There tends to be a lack of personal hygiene and the skin often looks sallow and as if there are numerous sores, perhaps from picking at the skin. There may be long periods of sleep when the drugs wear off. With **long term use**, there tends to be nervous picking behavior, excessive fear that people are trying to hurt them (paranoia), aggressive behavior, irritability, and periods of excessive sleep ("crashing") followed by severe bouts of depression. Teeth often become neglected and have cavities. These drugs are highly addictive, both psychologically and physically. Long use will usually result in significant weight loss, extreme fatigue, and a weakened immune system. Death from overdose can occur.

Cocaine: Also known as crack, coke, snow, gold dust, rock, freebase, snort, hubba bubba, and flake. Cocaine, like the amphetamines, is a stimulant. It comes from the leaves of the coca plant. The coca leaves themselves are often used in the form of a tea in South America for treating altitude sickness as a home remedy, but the form we deal with in the States is usually a white powder, though in the form of "crack cocaine" it is light tan and comes in tiny chips or pellet sized "rocks". Cocaine is potent and is usually inhaled or "snorted" into the nose. It can also be injected or smoked in the "free-base" form. Glass pipes are used to hold the "rock" while heat is applied and the fumes are inhaled. The drug reaches the brain in a matter of seconds and is very stimulating and very addicting. There is a very intense pleasure for a short time which is followed by depression and then a strong craving for more cocaine, often resulting in crime to gain a new supply of the drug. I recall one addict's comment to me that he was never able to achieve the high that he had on his first use, but in spite of that, he continued to try.

Signs of use include frequent sniffing in those users who "snort", since the drug tends to cause a "rebound" in the mucous membranes of the nose, resulting in a stuffy feeling in the user and a feeling of having to sniff to clear the nose. Rapid shifts occur in the mood of the user; the personality changes; aggressive behavior becomes prominent. With **long term use**, the person becomes addicted, there may be paranoia (though some people feel that the fears of both amphetamine and cocaine users are well founded, considering the seedy characters they associate with to get their drugs). Physical changes can occur resulting in increased heart rate and blood pressure, tremors, convulsions, and even stroke and death from cardiovascular accident or from overdose.

Barbiturates, Sedatives and Prescription drugs: also known as barbs, downers, yellow jackets, reds, quaaludes, "ludes", pennies, sleeping pills, and other numerous names. they tend to be depressants of central nervous system function as is alcohol. They most often come as pills or capsules, but may be ingested or injected into the veins or even smoked. They are frequently stolen from the medicine chest or from other peoples' homes. The symptoms and effects of the drugs are multiplied when taken with alcohol.

Barbiturates and sedatives are less commonly prescribed these days by doctors, but other forms of medicine which have taken their place are the **benzodiazepines**, a somewhat less dangerous group of drugs, but which can also be abused. In this class of drugs are included Valium, Librium, Xanax, Ativan, Klonopin, and Restoril. Their generic names sound similar to each other: diazepam, chlordiazepoxide, lorazepam, alprazolam, clonazepam, etc. Like the sedatives and barbiturates, they tend to be depressants and can be addicting.

They tend to come in pill form and are swallowed, and are usually taken from the medicine cabinet at home or at the homes of friends or in burglaries.

Signs of use are similar to alcohol and include confused and disoriented behavior, slurred speech, impaired motor skills, depression, irritability, and quick temper with argumentative tone. There is often drowsiness and long periods of sleep. Tolerance develops rather quickly, especially to barbiturates and the need for use of increased quantities develops rapidly.

Long term use usually leads to addiction and to depression. Convulsions, coma and death can occur from overdose. Withdrawal symptoms are similar to those of alcohol.

Inhalants: These are organic solvents. A solvent is something that will dissolve other substances. People use solvents to clean off organic materials from objects among other uses. Obviously, when used in the body, they can dissolve useful body materials and can cause major damage to vital organs. They can include gasoline, airplane glue, nail polish remover, lighter fluid, amyl nitrate in whipping cream cans, solvents like toluene, spray paint on rags and sniffed; just about any kind of organic compound. The fumes are usually inhaled after the substance has been placed on some form of cloth to produce intoxication. They are easy to obtain, but can be extremely dangerous to the user. Some fumes can cause temporary blindness, and most will cause damage to the lungs, brain, kidneys and liver. Death is possible from suffocation and heart failure.

Signs of use include feelings of excitement and exhilaration followed by a loss of coordination, distorted perceptions and extreme confusion. There is an appearance of intoxication as if drunk, speech may be slurred, nausea may be present. As with other intoxicants, there may be violence and lack of inhibitions.

Heroin and opioids: Heroin is a substance that is formed when morphine, a medicinal painkiller extracted from the oriental poppy, is altered to produce something which is 100 times more potent than the original morphine. In its pure form, heroin is a white powder that is illegal, even to medical doctors, and is sold on the streets. It is usually injected, but can be "snorted" or even smoked. Additionally "tar heroin", which is a dark brown sticky tar-like substance that smells like vinegar, is three to four times more potent than white heroin and is more popular on the streets. Other names for heroin include smack, "H", horse, hard stuff, white stuff, tar, tar heroin, gum, raw tar, chiva, and others. Other opioids, though not as potent as heroin, also have potential for abuse. They include morphine, codeine, and other synthetic prescription drugs such as demerol, talwin, hydrocodone, Dilaudid, oxycodone, Lortabs, Percodan, Tylox, Vicodin, and others.

Heroin is highly addictive, both psychologically and physically. As with cocaine, the addict's first and foremost need is the drug and anything that interferes with that goal must get out of the way. The drug replaces loyalties, families, loves, and careers.

Signs of use include constricted (small) pupils, flushing of the face, a dazed and far off look, and a feeling of well-being followed by drowsiness and apathy. Withdrawal symptoms occur usually about eight to fourteen hours after the last "fix" and include sweating, chills, yawning, muscle cramping, nausea, diarrhea, and runny nose. The symptoms somewhat resemble a severe flu or cold.

Long term use results in addiction, personality change, loss of judgment and loss of self control. There is often loss of appetite with weight loss. Sometimes delirium and anxiety occur, and there is always the risk of overdose and death. Since heroin is usually "cut" or diluted with other inert substances such as sugar, when an addict manages to get his/her hands on more "pure" or less diluted drug, he/she is used to injecting more than is needed in the more pure form and the result is overdose. Heroin is a central nervous system depressant, so too much allows the brain to "forget" to breathe, and as the person loses consciousness due to the effect of the drug, the person also forgets to breathe and does not have enough oxygen to sustain life.

210

Designer drugs: Makers of street drugs tend to try to beef up their product to get an edge on the competition, so they sometimes add substances to the product to give it an added kick. They "lace" it. Sometimes this can be extremely dangerous.

Substances that the user doesn't know about can cause great damage to the body. Also many manufacturers of illicit drugs are careless with the ingredients they use or take shortcuts in their production, resulting in impurities such as lead or other heavy metals getting into the drugs, also resulting in additional health hazards. In addition, makers of illicit drugs sometimes attempt to improve the "high" of drugs by chemical additions in the process of manufacturing them. The test cases are usually those "customers" on the street who try them out, and some of the outcomes can be deadly. **When drugs are purchased on the street, one never knows what one is really getting, or in what strength.**

Hallucinogens: These are essentially drugs which have become more prominent since the sixties. They produce a distortion of the senses and can produce visual, auditory and other sensory hallucinations. They vary in effect depending on the substance, so I will discuss several types of hallucinogen which are probably the most common.

LSD: Otherwise known as Lysergic Acid Diethylamide, is also known as "acid", 'cid, cubes, sugar, blotter acid, blotter, and microdot. Many of these names refer to the way the acid is used. Sometimes it is dropped as a liquid onto a cube of sugar, sometimes onto blotter paper. It can thus come in liquid form, in capsules, on a sugar cube, in a tablet or other form of pill, or on blotter paper, often segmented into dose units, like sheets of postage stamps, sometimes with cartoon characters printed on the paper. "Window pane" LSD is the crystalline form which is compressed into transparent sheets and resembles cellophane.

LSD is very potent in very small quantities. It is 100 times as potent as psilocybin, the psychoactive ingredient in "magic mushrooms". It was first discovered in 1938 by a chemist named Hoffman who was working with substances derived from a fungus in a laboratory. While working in the lab with LSD, he inhaled extremely small amounts of the substance and began to experience hallucinations. This occurred in 1943. It wasn't until the 1960's however, that it began to be used by those interested in its alteration of perceptual experiences. It was around this time that psychologist Timothy Leary, a credible academician at one time, espoused the use of LSD and coined the phrase, "Turn on, tune in, drop out." In addition, the counter-culture got into full swing, and anti-authoritarian attitudes toward the Viet Nam War were rampant. The Beatles with their anti-establishment message were rising in popularity.

Use of LSD is rarely for more than a week at a time, because tolerance develops so rapidly that the desired effect weakens. Also, mixing LSD with other hallucinogens like mescaline or psilocybin weakens the effect of the other drugs because of cross-tolerance.

Another bit of information: Morning Glory seeds contain lysergic acid derivatives, especially lysergic acid amide, a close relative of LSD. Usually the commercial packaging of these seeds in many varieties, including Heavenly Blue and Pearly Gates, also includes the treatment with insecticides, fungicides, and other toxic chemicals, so individuals who use these seeds as a raw material for the production of the drug, have already included additives which can be very detrimental to the health of the user.

Signs of use: These include dilated (large) pupils, increased blood pressure and heart rate, tremor, and increased body temperature. Visual and auditory hallucinations, anxiety, panic, and depression may occur, and often the inability to avoid physical harm because the ordinary reactions and defense mechanisms are disrupted. People under the influence of LSD have been known to jump off buildings thinking that they can fly, or walk into traffic thinking they are invincible.

Long term use includes the dangers of death from careless behavior and the risk of permanent insanity, which has been known to occur. In addition "flashbacks" or the re-experiencing of perceived events, including hallucinations, while under the influence has been known to occur as long as months and even years after the use of LSD. In addition there can be psychological dependence, personality changes, and possible brain changes or genetic damage. It would appear, however, that physical addiction does not develop.

Dimethyltryptamine (DMT) and Psilocybin (and psilocin) are substances that are in the same class of hallucinogen as LSD. Psilocybin is the more common and is derived from the Mexican mushroom (Psilocybe mexicana) otherwise known as the "magic" mushroom. It is not restricted in its growth to Mexico in spite of its name. Otherwise known as 'shrooms, or psychedelic mushrooms, it can be found readily in the Northwest at certain times of the year, and can easily be transported. It can be grown in damp dark areas and can be dried and stored in jars or in baggies. It produces similar effects to peyote (mescaline) which will also be mentioned. It is usually found in its dried form; the mushrooms are small and have a bitter, pungent flavor.

Signs of use include dilated (large) pupils, hallucinations, anxiety, panic, emotional instability, and unpredictable and irrational behavior. Poor judgment and careless behavior again come into the picture with these drugs.

Long term use, as with LSD, may result in psychological dependence, personality change, flashbacks, and possible brain damage or chromosomal (genetic) damage. Death due to careless behavior or poor judgment and insanity are clearly possible long term effects.

Regarding **insanity**, some professionals distinguish between schizophrenia and the insanity caused by these drugs. Some say that the drugs may cause the psychosis that would have occurred, to manifest at an earlier age, or that they may cause a psychosis that would have otherwise remained dormant and not appeared without the use of drugs, or that they may cause a relapse in persons who have had a psychotic episode and thus far have recovered. Whatever the reason, insanity or psychosis can occur and can result in severe disruption in the user's life.

Mescaline: This is another hallucinogen similar in effect to psiloybin but the parent substance is found in the Peyote cactus of the Southwest and has been used in religious practices of the Native Americans in that area for thousands of years. It comes from the "buttons" of the cactus, but is only 1/4000 as strong as psilocybin.

Other hallucinogens include a class called phenylisopropylamines and include,

DOM, MDA, and MDMA ("ecstasy"). These are all synthetically produced and are structurally related to amphetamines. They are sometimes referred to as "stimulant-hallucinogens". There are literally hundreds of analogues or related compounds which have been synthesized and sometimes are found on the streets as so-called "designer drugs".

Phencyclidine (PCP): Otherwise known as "angel dust", whack, hog, wet, ozone. It is also called dust, tac, tic, earth, green, KW, and sheets. Cigarettes laced with PCP are known as Sherms, Mores, SuperKools. Originally developed by a pharmaceutical company as an anesthetic, the use of PCP and related compounds cyclohexamine and ketamine produced a form of anesthesia in which patients appeared catatonic, open-mouthed and fixed, sightless staring, flat expression, rigid posturing and sometimes waxy flexibility (keeping the limbs in the position in which they were placed as would a wax figure). These anesthetics were thus dubbed "dissociative anesthetics". Despite the anesthetic advantages which these compounds allowed, they also had drawbacks. Up to half the patients subjected to these compounds developed severe reactions during surgery, including agitation and hallucinations. In addition, many patients went on to develop psychotic reactions which persisted beyond surgery from anywhere between twelve hours and ten days. Today PCP is used only in veterinary applications as well as its use as a street drug.

PCP as a street drug is smoked, sniffed, or swallowed. It comes in the form of a sticky, oily liquid or a powder. It is often applied in liquid form to marijuana cigarettes. The liquid form is often carried in dark brown bottles similar to those containing vanilla extract.

Signs of use include wide staring eyes or rapidly shifting eye movement and hallucinations. Insensitivity to pain is prominent. Bizarre and unpredictable behavior along with irritability, panic, euphoria, confusion, anxiety and forgetfulness is often present. There is a poor perception of time and distance.

Long term use may result in paranoid delusions, aggressive behavior, personality changes, withdrawn behavior. It may result in psychological dependence and may cause temporary brain damage that can last for years. Death can occur from irrational and careless behavior or from respiratory failure.

PCP is a compound which enters the body and goes to fat cells to be stored. It tends to stay with people for a long time in their fat cells. I recall the story of one individual who was hospitalized for PCP psychosis, began to recover, and one day decided while in the hospital to begin a diet and started to lose weight. Suddenly one day he had a recurrence of his old symptoms. As he began to mobilize and break down the fat from his fat cells, the PCP which had been stored there also began to mobilize and caused a resurgence of his symptoms.

Anabolic Steroids: These compounds are male hormones or derivatives of these hormones which tend to increase muscle strength and tone, and to increase athletic performance. They are forbidden in athletic competitions, but are sometimes obtained by aspiring young athletes who want to excel. They tend to have far reaching effects on the body, including decreasing size of primary sex organs, decrease in reproductive function, increasing acne, negative effects on the liver and heart, and increased aggressiveness. A review of medical literature suggests that elevations and relatively sudden drops of levels of serum (blood) steroid hormones can produce psychological effects similar to those produced by substances of abuse.

These hormones tend to produce euphoria and increased libido or sexual urge. They have also been linked to aggression in young males. Symptoms of anxiety, irritability, insomnia, hot flashes, sweats, loss of appetite, and muscle aches and pains have been observed when the blood levels of these hormones drop suddenly after high usage. Another group of symptoms including loss of energy, loss of ability to enjoy things, loss of interest in sex, and depressed mood with suicidal thoughts has been reported to occur with sudden withdrawal from the use of anabolic steroids. Widely reported in the lay literature is marked aggression and homicidal violence, sometimes referred to as "roid rage".

Signs of use: Any athletic appearing individual presenting with physical or psychological complaints should be considered as a possible user of anabolic steroids, but especially if the individual reports an obsessive interest in health, exercise, or weight lifting and spends excessive time periods in gyms or health clubs. Consumption of large amounts of vitamins and nutritional supplements is another clue. At the same time, there may be a reluctance to engage in any other drug use, including alcohol, out of a desire to live healthy. Many individuals will not admit to the use of steroids immediately. An overall appearance of muscularity is common. Females may show more hair than usual, even on the face. They may also have a deepened and coarse voice, small breasts, and an enlarged clitoris. Males may show increased male-pattern baldness, small testicles, and even enlargement of the breasts. Acne is more common, and individuals may complain of sore tendons and muscles and also difficulty in urinating.

Long term use may result in disruption of the endocrine (glands) system in the body. It may permanently affect the sex organs, growth, and the control of other important glands in the body. It may lead to depression, manic behavior, paranoia, hallucinations, or other psychosis. Toxic or poisonous effects on the heart are also possible, and electrocardiograms may be necessary to evaluate the condition of the heart.

AIDS (HIV virus): In this day and age the fear of pregnancy and even the old dreaded sexually transmitted diseases like syphilis, gonorrhea, lymphogranuloma venereum, and even herpes are not in the forefront when it comes to sexual activity without protection. In the teen population, there is always the concern that hormones go wild and kids think first with their sexual organs, then with their heads. This is especially true when their inhibitions are lowered by the use of drugs or alcohol. It is also true that since the HIV virus is transmitted by body fluids, unprotected sex is one way to aquire it, but sharing needles while using IV drugs is another way. The myth continues, however, that AIDS is a disease of gay men. It is true that the virus may be more easily transferred through the tissue present in the anus and colon, because of the makeup of that barrier compared to the lining of the vagina, but there are more and more heterosexual transmissions of AIDS as time goes on. Even if there had only been one previous sexual contact by a sexual partner, and that person had had only one previous sexual contact, one doesn't really know how many people that first partner slept with, and one may have had and passed on the virus. So, if you have had sex with a partner, you have in essence, slept with all of the remote sexual partners all the way back.

Teens tend not to be as concerned about their mortality as parents are. They do not necessarily think of the very real danger of the AIDS epidemic. If they are going to be participating in sexual activity, they should be using condoms (which clearly are not 100% safe) whether or not they are already protected by birth control of some other sort. They should also know the dangers of sharing needles, so that if they do get involved in IV drug use, they will at least know not to add the increased danger that goes with needle sharing.

Hepatitis: In this day of AIDS we often forget about potentially life-threatening infections that can be and are easily aquired by the careless use of needles and blood products. We don't want to forget hepatitis, which, if it doesn't kill a person, often disables him for a long period of time, and can cause permanent damage to a person's liver, resulting in disability for a lifetime for some individuals.

Drug-related psychosis: This is a group of psychotic disorders that are related to drugs, some short-lived, some persistent or even permanent. What this means is that when using drugs, the kid goes crazy and stays that way for a short time, a long time, or permanently.

The first type that I will talk about is **pathological intoxication**. This is a situation that occurs with alcohol, when just a small amount to drink can trigger a response that is exaggerated and the individual becomes irrational, paranoid, or delusional. It usually clears with detoxification from the alcohol, but may return with small amounts to drink.

Use of marijuana and other hallucinogens can also cause delusional and/or paranoid thinking. I recently saw a young man who was tormented by the intense belief that his thoughts were "out loud" and that people around him could hear what he was thinking. This occurred shortly after using marijuana. He began to come around with the help of antipsychotic medicine, but again used marijuana and the feelings started all over again, and worse. I have seen similar situations with marijuana, and have come to tell these people that they have to treat this drug as though they were allergic to it.

Other drugs will have as their main effect a psychotic-like picture. Most of the hallucinogenic drugs will do this. LSD, mescaline, psilocybin and phencyclidine all tend to distort reality and this is the main reason they are used, however, they can also leave permanent residuals in some individuals. One just can never know just who these individuals will be, so it is like an unlucky lottery.

Amphetamines are notorious for causing a severe depression when "coming down" off them, but in people who continuously use them for extended periods, **they tend to induce a severe paranoia** that is not just the "looking over your shoulder" type of wariness that comes naturally to the sleazy crowd who use the stuff, but a severe paranoia that is virtually impossible to distinguish from acute paranoid schizophrenia, even by well-trained psychiatrists. Often these people have to be hospitalized for several days to a week until the speed is out of their systems, and their psychotic symptoms begin to clear. Sometimes they do not clear, but remain psychotic.

Thus, in addition to the immediate effects of drug use and abuse, one can be hampered temporarily or permanently by the residual effects of these dangerous drugs.

Family intervention: In order for families to intervene in drug problems, the first order of business is to identify that there is a problem. Some of the signs of drug and alcohol use were listed above. When a change in personality or manner of doing things becomes apparent, it is time to look into why. The next step is to do some **detective work** to find out just what is going on. Sometimes a good friend who is no longer hanging around with the teen is a good source of information. Sometimes pieces can be put together with school personnel. It may be that other things are the issue, but if it is still suspicious, it is time to confront the individual with the changes and concerns of others around him. **Confrontation** is done best when a number of people who all have some piece of this person's life are involved. Parents, teachers, girlfriend, buddies, other relatives, bosses, etc., are all good people to involve, since the more people and the more who are influential in his life, the more difficult it is to deny the problem.

The next step is to get an **assessment** for drug and/or alcohol use by a professional who is reasonably qualified in the field. Usually this means someone who is experienced in the area of drug and alcohol treatment. It may include drug testing by a physician. Often this individual will know of **available resources** in the area that will fit the need for the level of problem that has presented to that professional. Finally, it is up to the parents to be **firm** in insisting on treatment, since the nature of this type of illness is **denial** and the child will usually get into a **bargaining** mode. Once you start to give in to the bargaining, you are on the way to losing the battle. You need to be loving but firm, caring but unbending, and patient but consistent. Remember that your child does not need to like you at the moment, that to love him is to let him be angry with you for your caring, but not to let him abuse you. Loving and liking is often two very different things altogether. When drugs are the relationship that your child has chosen, he will find that all other relationships will take a back seat to that one. It is not until he is divorced from the drugs that any level of trust will again develop, and the divorce must be very cold before other relationships can be trusted very well.

Our goal in this chapter has been to familiarize you with the difficulties of drug use and its impact on families. Hopefully, you will not have to deal with this problem, but many of you will. Do not shut your eyes to this possibility, because if it gets a good hold on your kid, it is a tough one from which to extricate him.

Pearls For Parents:

1) You can always tell when an addict is lying, because his lips will be moving.

2) If there is a fairly sudden change in personality or pattern of behavior, look for the reason. It may be drugs.

3) If things start showing up that don't seem to be there for a good reason, e.g., excess money, things that are expensive, with no really good explanation about how they were gotten (other than a friend gave them as a gift) be suspicious. Don't be afraid to question vigorously. Don't buy into the "you don't trust me" routine. Your job as a parent is not to trust unless there is a clearly demonstrated reason to do so. If things aren't right, it is your job to investigate until you are satisfied.

4) Sudden shift from great grades and performance at school or in sports to a lackluster style should raise the red flags.

5) Sudden shift in peer group to kids that you don't feel comfortable with—little eye contact, avoidance of interaction with you as parents, reluctance to give out much straightforward information, etc.

6) Remember, if your kids are not angry with you some of the time, you are probably not doing your job. The most difficult thing for a parent is to shift from being a friend to your child to being a manager, at a moment's notice.

7) Kids learn most by modeling, not what you tell them. It's what you do, not what you say.

MOVIES AND BOOKS:
Classic Movies:
"Clean and Sober" (Michael Keaton)
"Drugstore Cowboy" (Matt Dillon)
"Days of Wine and Roses" (Jack Lemmon, Lee Remick)
"Lost Weekend" (Ray Milland)
"Barfly" (Michael Rourke, Fay Dunaway)
"Call Me Anna" (Patty Duke)
"Darkness Before Dawn"
"Not My Kid"
"Under The Influence"
"Sarah T: Portrait of a Teenage Alcoholic"
"Sid and Nancy"
"Only When I Laugh" (Kristy McNichol, Marsha Mason)

Books:
Kids and Drugs— A Handbook for Parents and Professionals
by Joyce M. Tobias R.N. 2nd edition
Panda Press Annandale VA 22003

Al-Anon Family Groups (formerly "Living With An Alcoholic")
www.al-anon.alateen.org
Al-Anon Family Group Headquarters, Inc.
New York 1991

Alcoholics Anonymous www.aa.org
Alcoholic Anonymous World Services, Inc.
New York City 1976—3rd edition

Alateen - One Day at a Time
Al-Anon Family Group Headquarters, Inc.
New York 1994

Pamphlets:
These are all available through the
Al-Anon Family Group Headquarters, Inc.
P.O. Box 862, Midtown Station
New York, NY 10018-0862
212-302-7240

"Operation Alateen"
"Facts About Alateen"
"Alcoholism The Family Disease"
"Youth and the Alcoholic Parent"
"A Guide for the Family of the Alcoholic"
"Twelve Steps and Twelve Traditions for Alateen"
"To The Mother And Father Of An Alcoholic"
"How Can I Help My Children?"
"Al-Anon Family Treatment Tool in Alcoholism"
"Getting in Touch with Al-Anon/Alateen"

Wikipedia List of Addiction and Substance Abuse Organizations

CHAPTER 11:
THEY'RE BACK!!!

"Home is the place where, when you have to go there,
They have to take you in."
—Robert Frost "The Death of the Hired Man"

The **economics** of this day and age are a lot different from that of the baby boomers growing up. In our day, scholarships were relatively easy to get, loans were available for school with easy payback terms, and when you got a college education, you were pretty well assured of getting a job. Today's kids—another story. Even if there were loans to get, completing a college degree does not guarantee that you will be able to pay them back. Thus it is up to parents more and more to help out.

Most kids find themselves out in an apartment sooner or later after graduation from high school. Many of these kids also tend to move back home, because they just cannot afford to live out there on their own. When they do, the natural tendency is for them to become ten years old again. They once again leave their dishes on the counter or in the sink and their clothes and other miscellaneous paraphernalia lying around. They leave their half-finished food items for someone else to pick up. They come in at all hours without regard for the sleep of those who have to get up and go to work. It is **the old habit of being home again**.

One of the problems is that being out of the home does not break the old habit of being a kid. The other problem is that this kid is really no longer a kid. Parents, too, have developmental stages, and one of them is when their kids reach the age when they should either be working toward a degree past high school or getting a full-time job. There is, I believe, an innate urge on the part of parents to shoo their kids out the door to a productive life, and when they come home from work to see their kid lying on the couch watching TV, there is something enraging about that. The word that comes most easily to mind is **jettison**. It's like, "Launch that kid to something productive that has a future." It takes a great deal of patience on the part of parents to not become the year-round grinch, finding fault with a myriad of small and often petty circumstances.

How do we prevent such a situation? It is likely to happen that one or more kid may need shelter and food, a place to park the beater car, to borrow the gas card from time to time, to borrow the tent and sleeping bag for a campout, or whatever, so it is important to **plan ahead** just a bit.

Most important is to set up **ground rules and expectations** before they move back. Don't wait until they have settled in. Let them know that there are things that you will want them to do on a regular basis, usually the least of which is to pick up after themselves, including clothes and dishes, and to put things back where they found them after using them. Keeping their own areas clean is also very helpful. **Boundaries** are very important. They shouldn't be taking or using things without checking first that it is OK. They should be told what is OK and what is not. A good rule of thumb is the **"room-mate rules"** concept. If you wouldn't treat a room-mate that way, don't even consider doing it to your parents. Be respectful about noise and time of day, for example. Don't borrow my shirt or dress without asking. I may have wanted to wear it myself for something special. Another important item is the notion of **time limits**. Try to set some time limit on how long they plan to stay and what your expectations are about that time frame. It will help you to deal with the "temporariness" of the return home and the fact that they will eventually get on with their lives. It will happen. It just feels like it never will occur.

Leaving on good terms is an important goal. It is always easier to go away angry, especially if it is hard to go. Work hard at making the eventual departure in a good spirit. The kid should know that even if his parents have a need to get into another stage in their lives, as does the kid, that the invitation is still open for him to visit and spend time there. It is just that the time needs to be planned ahead, so the parents can look forward to it. That way the kid can continue to feel loved and welcome, and that way the parents don't have to deal with surprises, which at this stage of their lives, they may not be very good at.

Pearls For Parents:

1) No, money still doesn't grow on trees.

2) No, Mary Poppins doesn't live here anymore.

3) You don't want me to bore you with telling you how it was for me at your age again, do you?

4) Periodically ask about their plans. That begins to plant the seed that they should have some.

5) A good general rule is: If you are not going to school, you need to have a job and work to contribute to the food and rent, as best you can, but you still need to pick up after yourself as well, just as we do.

Resources:

1) The local college academic advising office for those who are considering attending, but don't know where to start.
2) The local unemployment office for job opportunities.
3) Friends who may have leads or a business and could hire them.
4) Newspaper want ads.

Chapter 12:
ONE LAST LOOK

"Oh brave new world, that has such people in it."
—Shakespeare "The Tempest"

We have attempted to give an overview of the teenage years, with a look at the normal developmental process, communication, relationships with family, peers, work and school. We have looked at abnormal behavior, use of drugs and alcohol, mental health and disability problems, sexuality in teens, religious and moral issues, and the economic issues that force our kids to come back to us for help. As I mentioned in the opening chapter of this book, it is not an encyclopedia and would not be a useful book to parents if we tried to make it so. We have included, as much as we could, a variety of resources at the end of each chapter that might be helpful, and have included movies and novels as well as self-help books, that might add more insight to what adolescents are experiencing.

We do want you to remember that teens are not all in turmoil, but they are all making some mistakes, as we are (as we wing it through parenthood, as our parents did before us), learning mistakes for all of us. I cannot emphasize enough that it is important that our kids see us as recognizing our own mistakes and learning from them, as we expect them to do. Modeling is the best means of teaching, and our main job, as I have emphasized in this book, is as teachers, teaching our kids to be safe enough to survive and to be properly intimate. Modeling how we deal with our mistakes is one of the best ways to teach our kids how to deal with theirs.

Teens are good people. They usually try in one form or another to live up to our expectations. They are also learning to think for themselves. I would like to share what one 15 year old girl wrote to her aunt, who shared it with me. I found out later that she had taken the main idea from a book called, <u>Chicken Soup for the Teenage Soul</u>, by Jack Canfield, Mark Victor Hansen and Kimberly Kirberger. However she had changed a lot of the content and put in her own words, which follow:

LIFE

Life isn't about keeping score.
It's not about how many friends you have
Not about if you have plans this weekend
Or if you're alone.

It isn't about who you've dated,
Who you used to date,
How many people you've dated
Or if you haven't been with anyone at all.

It isn't about who you have kissed, it's not about sex.
It isn't about who your family is or how much money they have
Or what kind of car you drive.
Or where you were sent to school.
It's not about how beautiful or ugly you are.
Or what clothes you wear, what shoes you have on,
Or what kind of music you listen to.
It's not about if your hair is blond, red, black, or brown
Or if your skin is too light or too dark.

Not about what grades you get,
How smart you are
How smart everybody else thinks you are,
Or how smart standardized tests say you are.

It's not about what clubs you're in
Or how good you are at your "sport".
It's not about representing your whole being on a piece of paper
And seeing who will "accept the written you".

LIFE JUST ISN'T

But, life is about who you love and who you hurt.
It's about who you make happy or unhappy purposefully.
It's about keeping or betraying trust.
It's about friendship, used as a sanctity or a weapon.

It's about what you say and mean, maybe hurtful, maybe heartening.
About starting rumors and contributing to petty gossip.
It's about what judgments you pass and why.
And who your judgments are spread to.

It's about who you've ignored with full control and intention.
It's about jealousy, fear, ignorance, and revenge.
It's about carrying inner hate and love,
Letting it grow, and spreading it.

But most of all,
It 's about using your life
To touch or poison people's hearts in such a way
That could have never occurred alone.

Only you choose the way those hearts are affected,
And those choices are what life's all about.

About the Authors

Jerome C. Vergamini M.D.
PHYSICIAN
Distinguished Life Fellow of the American Psychiatric Association.
Diplomate of the AmericanBoard of Psychiatry and Neurology

Completed training in psychiatry followed by service in the
U.S. Air force for 2 years followed by 3 ½ years of service
to the state of Wisconsin. Then completed 2 more years
of training in child and adolescent psychiatry.

Practiced many years in a variety of settings, including
private practice as well as consulting to approximately
twenty different children's treatment programs.

Served as president of the Oregon Psychiatric Association
and on the board of same for 9 years.

SPECIAL AWARDS:
"Award of Appreciation" from Eugene Education Association--1980
Service to Education Award" from Oregon Education Association--1980
Awarded "Distinguished Life Fellowship in the American Psychiatric Association
January 1, 2003

Married since 1965 to Judy Vergamini. We are both adoptive and birth parents. We have three children. We are also now grandparents.

Ray Miskimins, Ph.D.
LICENSED CLINICAL PSYCHOLOGIST
Married 54 years with 3 children, 2 boys and 1 girl. Has a
Master's degree and a Ph.D. both in psychology.
Member of PsyChi National Honorary Society in Psychology and of the American
Psychological Association.

Has worked in a variety of capacities including as a clinic administrator, a research coordinator and consultant, and as an associate professor. He has also worked in private practice and as a director of an adolescent inpatient residential setting.

Has published numerous professional articles as well as other books on such topics as whitewater rafting, mountain biking, tennis, table tennis, and guitar playing, as well as a children's book called, "The Great Yellow Beebleberry".

Among other avocations, has been the owner of a jewelry making shop, the owner of a bicycle shop, and a business called, "Photography of the West". Also in his repertoire is coaching tennis and table tennis.

<u>**UNANSWERED QUESTIONS**</u>: As we mentioned in the first part of this book, it cannot be an all-inclusive encyclopedia or compendium of adolescence. If we have been successful, there will be a lot of questions or concerns that may continue to need to be addressed in yet another way. For this reason, we will provide a special email address where questions or other issues might be forwarded. We would hope such information could be addressed in a future follow-up book. Thank you. We hope that this book has proven to be helpful in understanding and providing useful information for you and your teens.

Send your questions to:
FieldGuideQuestions@ecojusticepress.com

9 781945 432095